WHOLE 30 COOKBOOK
120 Fast and Easy Recipes For Your Whole 30

Table of Contents

Introduction

Chapter 1 Whole30

Chapter 2 Breakfast Recipes

Chapter 3 Appetizers

Chapter 4 Salads Recipes

Chapter 5 Bowl Meals

Chapter 6 Main Dishes

Chapter 7 Side Dishes

Chapter 8 Dessert Recipes

Conclusion

Introduction

Do you want to make healthier food choices that would lead to natural weight loss? If you have been struggling with restrictive eating plans and finding it hard to lose weight, then the Whole30 eating plan is for you. Eating healthy, nutritious food doesn't have to be complicated. This simple change in lifestyle will not only help you improve your physical health but your psychological health as well. With this eating program, you will improve your immune and cardiovascular health and lower the risk of chronic diseases. Each recipe in this book has been carefully tested and includes only fresh, unprocessed meats, vegetables, herbs, and spices.

Hectically busy lifestyles often force us to consume processed and ready-to-eat foods. These foods contain artificial preservatives, colorings, flavorings that increase inflammation. This is why people who consume these foods are likely to suffer from diseases like heart problem, high blood pressure, diabetes, and obesity. Whether you are a first-time Whole30 follower or an expert, this cookbook will provide you with plenty of delicious recipes. In this very manuscript you will find eating healthier a joy rather than a chore. This specific volume will have you prepare sophisticated and amazing meals with complete ease.

☐ **Copyright 2018 by STEVE NOLAN - All rights reserved.**

Chapter 1 Whole30

The whole30 concept conveys that certain food groups (such as dairy, grains, sugar, and legumes) can have a negative effect on your health and overall quality of life. The whole30 helps you heal and recovers from the negative effects of these foods. With whole30, you will boost your metabolism, lower inflammation and enjoy a disease-free, healthy body.

The whole30 rules:

- Can't consume added sugar of any kind
- Can't consume alcohol in any form
- Can't eat grains
- Can't eat legumes
- Can't eat dairy
- Can't consume MSG or other added ingredients

What you can eat:

- Meat
- Poultry
- Fish
- Fruits
- Fats

These cooking ingredients are allowed during your Whole30:

- Clarified butter or ghee

- Fruit juice as a sweetener
- Green beans and snow/snap peas
- Vinegar
- Coconut aminos
- Iodized salt

With a few steps, you can make Whole30 cheaper:
- Chop your own everything.
- Make your own everything.
- Prep your own emergency food.
- Buy spices in bulk.
- Buy frozen meat, seafood, vegetables or fruit.
- Skip expensive toppings such as nuts, seeds or bacon bits.

If you want to cook fast:
- Buy pre-cut or spiral-sliced vegetables.
- Buy whole30 approved condiments.
- Make your own broth.
- Roast your own chicken.
- Use dried herbs.
- Use minced garlic or ginger from a jar.

Chapter 2 Breakfast Recipes

Scrambled Eggs

Prep time: 10 minutes	Cook time: 10 minutes	Servings: 2

Ingredients

- Cooking fat – 2 tbsp.
- Onion – ½, finely chopped
- Bell pepper – ½, any color, cut into strips
- Sliced mushrooms – 1 cup
- Chopped greens – 1 cup (kale, spinach, chard)
- Large eggs – 6, beaten
- Avocado – 1, split lengthwise, pitted, peeled and diced
- Salt – ¼ tsp.

- Black pepper – ¼ tsp.

Method

1. Heat a large skillet over medium-low heat.
2. Add the cooking fat and add the onion, bell pepper and mushrooms. Cook and stir for 4 to 5 minutes or until onions are translucent.
3. Stir in the greens and cook until they begin to wilt. Add the eggs and cook and stir for 5 to 7 minutes, or until the eggs are scrambled, and fluffy.
4. Remove the pan from the heat.
5. Top with diced avocado, season with salt and pepper and serve.

Southwest Scrambled Eggs

| Prep time: 15 minutes | Cook time: 5 to 7 minutes | Servings: 2 |

Ingredients

- Avocado – 1, split, lengthwise, pitted, and peeled
- Cooking fat – 2 tbsp.
- Large eggs – 6, beaten
- Salt – 1 tsp.
- Black pepper – ½ tsp.
- Salsa – 1 cup

Method

1. Cut the avocado halves into slices.
2. Heat the cooking fat in a large skillet over medium heat.

3. In a bowl, whisk the eggs with salt and pepper.
4. When the oil is hot, add the eggs. Cook and stir for 5 to 7 minutes, or until the eggs are scrambled and fluffy.
5. Divide the eggs between 2 plates.
6. Top with avocado, and spoon the salsa over both portions.
7. Serve.

Spinach Frittata

Prep time: 10 minutes	Cook time: 10 to 15 minutes	Servings: 2

Ingredients

- Large eggs – 6, beaten
- Salt – ¼ tsp.
- Black pepper – ¼ tsp.
- Cooking fat – 2 tbsp.
- Onion – ½, diced
- Diced seeded tomato – 1 cup, plus a few slices as a topping
- Baby spinach – 1 (9 ounces) bag, roughly chopped
- Grated zest and juice of ¼ lemon

Method

1. Preheat the oven to 500F.
2. In a bowl, whisk the eggs with salt and pepper.
3. Heat a large skillet over medium heat. Add the cooking fat and add onion and tomato to the pan. Cook and stir for 2 to 3 minutes, or until softened.
4. Add the spinach and let it wilt for 30 seconds. Add the eggs and fold them into the vegetables.
5. Cook without stirring for 3 to 4 minutes or until the eggs are firm.
6. Place a few tomato slices on top.
7. Drizzle with the lemon juice and sprinkle the lemon zest over the top.
8. Transfer the pan with the eggs to the oven and bake in the oven until the top is golden brown, about 3 to 5 minutes.
9. Cut into slices and serve.

Eggs and Sausage Breakfast

Prep time: 5 to 10 minutes	Cook time: 15 to 20 minutes	Servings: 2

Ingredients

- Cooking fat – 3 tbsp.
- Finley diced white onion – ¼ cup
- Ground meat – ½ pound (pork, turkey, chicken)
- Dried sage – ¼ tsp.
- Salt - ¼ tsp.
- Black pepper – 1/8 tsp.
- Garlic powder – 1/8 tsp.
- Sweet potato – 1, peeled and cut into large dice
- Bell pepper – ½, seeded, ribs removed and diced

- Large eggs – 4, cracked into a bowl

Method

1. Preheat the oven to 350F. Line a baking sheet with parchment paper.
2. Heat 1 tbsp. of cooking fat in a large heavy skillet over medium heat. Add the onion and cook and stir for 2 minutes or until softened.
3. Transfer the onion to a mixing bowl and add the ground meat, sage, salt, pepper, and garlic powder.
4. Form the mixture into 4 equal patties.
5. Cook the sausage until browned, about 2 minutes per side.
6. Add the sausage to a baking sheet and bake in the oven for 5 to 7 minutes, or until sausage is no longer pink in the middle.
7. Add 1 tbsp. cooking fat to the same skillet and cook all 4 eggs for 5 to 8 minutes. Cook slowly and keep the yolk-side up.
8. Arrange the sausage patties and eggs on 2 plates and serve.

Seared Salmon Benedict

| Prep time: 15 minutes | Cook time: 10 minutes | Servings: 2 |

Ingredients

- Salmon fillets – 2 (5 ounces each) skin removed
- Salt – 1 tsp.
- Black pepper – ½ tsp.
- Cooking fat – 3 tbsp.
- Large eggs – 2, poached
- Hollandaise – ½ cup
- Cayenne pepper – 1 pinch

Method

1. Preheat the oven to 350F.
2. Season both sides of the salmon with salt and pepper.
3. In a large skillet, heat the cooking fat over medium-high heat.
4. Add the salmon fillets in the hot oil, skin side down.
5. Sear the salmon for 3 to 4 minutes.
6. Transfer the pan to the oven and bake for 5 to 7 minutes. Time depends on the thickness of the fillet.
7. Transfer the cooked salmon to a plate.
8. Place the poached eggs over the salmon and drizzle evenly with hollandaise.
9. Top with a dash of black pepper and serve.

Grain-Free Oatmeal

| Prep time: 5 minutes | Total time: 10 minutes | Servings: 1 |

Ingredients

- Medium apple – ½, sliced
- Date – 1
- Chia seeds – 1 tbsp.
- Unsweetened coconut – 1 tbsp.
- Slivered almonds - 1 tbsp.
- Almond butter for the topping
- Cashew milk for serving

Method

1. Chop the date and apple into small pieces.
2. Place them in a food processor. Add almonds, coconut and chia seeds.
3. Pulse until the mixture is similar to oatmeal.
4. Spoon the mixture into a bowl.
5. Top with milk and almond butter.
6. Stir and serve.

Zucchini Oatmeal

| Prep time: 5 minutes | Cook time: 10 minutes | Servings: 1 |

Ingredients

- Egg whites – ¾ cup
- Unsweetened almond milk – ¾ cup
- Ground flaxseed – 1 ½ tbsp.
- Large ripe banana – ½, mashed
- Zucchini – ½, grated
- Cinnamon – ½ tsp.

Method

1. In a bowl, combine zucchini and mashed banana. Set aside.

2. In a saucepan, combine almond milk and egg whites.
3. Heat over medium heat and stir with a spatula.
4. Add flaxseed and continue to mix until the mixture starts to thicken.
5. Add the zucchini-banana mixture and mix until the mixture thickens.
6. Sprinkle with cinnamon, lower heat and continue to stir.
7. Remove from heat.
8. Spoon in a bowl. Top with nuts, berries, nut butter and enjoy.

Banana Chia Pudding

| Prep time: 35 minutes | Total time: 35 minutes | Servings: 6 |

Ingredients

- Water – 1 cup
- Chia seeds – 2 ½ tbsp.
- Ripe bananas – 2
- Coconut milk – 1 cup, full fat
- Ground cinnamon – ½ tsp.
- Pinch salt

Method

1. To make the chia gel: In a bowl, add water and chia seeds. Mix with a spoon. Set aside for 30 minutes and occasionally mix with a spoon to break up any lumps.

2. To make the banana pudding: combine coconut milk and bananas in a food processor and mix until smooth.

3. Pour the mixture into a bowl. Mix in the chia gel, salt, and cinnamon.

4. Keep in the refrigerator and serve cold.

Coconut Smoothie

| Prep time: 5 minutes | Total time: 5 minutes | Servings: 1 |

Ingredients

- Coconut milk – 1 cup
- Pumpkin puree – ¼ cup
- Pumpkin pie spice – 2 tsp.
- Frozen banana – 1 sliced
- Ice – 1 cup

Method

1. In a blender, add the ice, banana, pumpkin, milk, and spice.

2. Bled on high speed until smooth.
3. Enjoy.

Banana Cherry Smoothie Bowl

Prep time: 5 minutes	Total time: 5 minutes	Servings: 1

Ingredients

- Frozen banana – 1
- Frozen cherries – 1 cup
- Almond butter – 1 tbsp.
- Unsweetened coconut flake – 1 tbsp.
- Almond milk – ½ cup
- For toppings – flaked coconut, chia seeds, granola, almond butter, and fresh cherries

Method

1. Combine the almond milk, coconut, almond butter, cherries and banana in a blender. Mix until smooth.

2. Transfer to a bowl, top with toppings and serve.

Sweet Potato Breakfast Bowl

| Prep time: 5 minutes | Total time: 5 minutes | Servings: 2 |

Ingredient

- Sweet potato – 1, baked and very hot
- Eggs – 2, whisked
- Ripe banana – 1, peeled
- Ghee – 1 tbsp.
- Cinnamon – ¼ tsp.
- Sea salt to taste
- Toppings: blueberries, figs, cherries, raisins, coconut butter, coconut cream

Method

1. Steam the sweet potato in the instant pot (about 16 minutes).

2. Make sure the sweet potato is very hot, then peel it.

3. Combine the whisked eggs and sweet potato in a medium bowl. Mash until the mixture is mixed well. Your aim is to cook the eggs with the very hot sweet potato.

4. Add the ghee, banana, cinnamon and season with salt. Mash again.

5. Top with toppings and serve.

Almond and Pumpkin Breakfast Porridge

Prep time: 5 minutes	Total time: 10 minutes	Servings: 1

Ingredients

- Canned pumpkin – 1 cup
- Almond pulp – 1/3 cup
- Ground flax or chia seed – 1 tbsp.
- Almond milk – 1/3 cup
- Pinch sea salt
- Ground cinnamon – ½ tsp.
- Maple syrup – 2 tsp.
- Toppings: dried fruit, cacao nibs, and chopped nuts

Method

1. In a saucepan, add the almond milk, sea salt, cinnamon, chia meal, pulp, and pumpkin.
2. Whisk over medium heat until the mixture bubbles.
3. Lower the heat and simmer for a few minutes. Stirring frequently.
4. Remove from the heat and drizzle with maple syrup.
5. Sprinkle with toppings and serve.

Turkey, Spinach Breakfast Frittata

Prep time: 20 minutes	Cook time: 10 minutes	Servings: 2 to 3

Ingredients

- Extra virgin olive oil – 2 tbsp.
- Garlic – 1 clove
- Ground turkey breast – 4 ounces
- Fresh asparagus – ½ cup
- Fresh baby spinach leaves – 1 cup, chopped

- Large eggs – 4
- Water – 1 tbsp.
- Snipped fresh dill – 2 tsp.
- Snipped fresh parsley – 1 tbsp.

Method

1. Preheat the broiler with the oven rack positioned 4 inches from the heating element.
2. Heat 1 tbsp. olive oil in an oven-safe skillet over medium heat.
3. Add garlic and cook and stir until golden.
4. Add the ground turkey and sprinkle with pepper.
5. Cook and stir for 3 to 4 minutes or until the meat is browned and cooked through. Break up the meat with a wooden spoon.
6. Transfer cooked turkey to a bowl. Set aside.
7. Return skillet to stovetop. Pour the remaining 1 tbsp. olive oil into the skillet.
8. Add asparagus and cook and stir over medium heat unit tender.
9. Stir in the cooked turkey and the spinach. Cook for 1 minute.
10. In a medium bowl, beat eggs with the water and the dill.
11. Pour egg mixture over turkey mixture in the skillet.
12. Cook and stir for 1 minute.

13. Transfer skillet to oven and broil for 3 to 4 minutes or until eggs are set and the top is browned.

14. Sprinkle with snipped parsley and serve.

Sweet Potato Hash Browns

Prep time: 8 minutes	Cook time: 8 to 10 minutes	Servings: 3 (6 hash browns)

Ingredients

- o   Medium sweet potatoes – 4, boiled
- o   Eggs – 1, beaten
- o   Scallions – 4, thinly chopped
- o   Ground almonds – 5 tbsp.
- o   Himalayan pink salt

- Freshly ground black pepper
- Olive oil or coconut oil – 2 tbsp.

Method

1. Once the sweet potato is soft right through, add it to the other ingredients and mash them all together.
2. Heat the oil in a pan over medium heat and form the mix into patties. Don't make them too thick.
3. Add them to the pan to cook.
4. Flatten in the pan with a spatula and cook for 4 minutes on each side or until golden and crispy.
5. Serve with eggs for breakfast.

Eggs in Avocado Boats

Prep time: 5 minutes	Cook time: 10 to 15 (microwave time 8 minutes)	Servings: 1

Ingredients

- Medium or large avocado – 1
- Small eggs – 2
- Himalayan pink salt
- Freshly ground black pepper
- Sprinkle of garlic powder
- Coconut oil – 1 tbsp.
- Cherry tomatoes – 1 handful
- Spinach – 1 handful
- Fresh cilantro

Method

1. Preheat the oven to 350F.
2. Halve the avocado, remove the stone and slice a little off the bottom so each half will lay flat on a baking tray.
3. Remove a little more avocado flesh to ensure there is enough room for the egg.
4. Add one egg to each half and season with garlic, salt, and pepper. Place them on a baking tray in the oven for 10 to 15 minutes.
5. When the eggs are around 5 minutes from being cooked, heat the coconut oil in a frying pan over medium heat and add the tomatoes. Cook until the tomatoes soften, then add the spinach and sauté.
6. Ensure the eggs are fully cooked before serving with the tomatoes and spinach.
7. Sprinkle the cilantro over the top and serve.

Chapter 3 Appetizers

Tuna Salad Cucumber Bites

Prep time: 10 minutes	Total time: 10 minutes	Servings: 4

Ingredients

- Tuna – 2 (5 oz.) cans
- Broccoli slaw – ½ cup, roughly chopped
- Diced red onion – 1/3 cup
- Diced bell pepper – ½ cup
- Fresh basil – ¼ cup, chopped

- Dry roasted cashews – ¼ cup, roughly chopped
- Lemon – 1, juiced
- Mayo – 1/3 to ½ cup
- Sea salt and black pepper to taste
- Medium cucumber – 1, sliced

Method

1. Except for the cucumber slices, combine everything in a bowl.
2. Top tuna salad on cucumber slices.
3. Garnish with chopped cashews and fresh basil.
4. Serve.

Cheese Pizza Kale Chips

| Prep time: 15 minutes | Total time: 90 minutes | Servings: 10 |

Ingredients

- Kale – 1 large bunch, (remove the stems, take only leaves) washed and pat dried
- Raw cashews – 2 cups, soaked overnight
- Jarred roasted pepper – 2/3 cup, and 3 tbsp. of the juice
- Nutritional yeast – 1/3 cup
- Olive oil – 3 tbsp.
- Lemon – 1, juiced
- Italian seasoning – 1 tbsp.

- Garlic powder – ½ tsp.
- Chili powder – ¼ tsp.
- Sea salt – ¼ tsp.
- Black pepper – ¼ tsp.

Method

1. Line 2 large baking sheets with foil, set aside.
2. Preheat the oven to 200F.
3. Place the kale leaves in a large bowl.
4. Process the remaining ingredients in a food processor until smooth.
5. Add the sauce to the bowl. Coat the kale leaves with the mixture.
6. Place the coated leaves on the baking sheets in a single layer.
7. Bake for 1 hour. Then flip and bake until dry and crispy, about 30 to 40 minutes more.
8. Serve.

Guacamole Deviled Eggs

| Prep time: 15 minutes | Total time: 15 minutes | Servings: 4 |

Ingredients

- Hard-boiled eggs – 6, egg yolks are separated and the white part is sliced in half, lengthwise
- Avocado – 1 medium
- Chopped red onion – 1 tbsp.
- Chopped cilantro – 1 tbsp.
- Lime juice – 1 to 2 tsp.
- Granulated garlic – ½ tsp.
- Cumin – ½ tsp.

- Chili powder – ¼ tsp.
- Sea salt – ¼ tsp. and more to taste
- Roma tomato – 1, finely diced

Method

1. Mash the egg yolks in a bowl.
2. Add the avocado flesh in the egg yolk bowl and mash well.
3. Mix in the chili powder, salt, cumin, garlic, lime juice, cilantro, and onion. Taste and adjust the seasoning.
4. Add the diced tomatoes and mix well.
5. Spoon the mixture into the egg whites.
6. Sprinkle with herbs or spices.
7. Serve.

Cauliflower Buffalo Bites

| Prep time: 10 minutes | Cook time: 20 minutes | Servings: 6 |

Ingredients

- Cauliflower florets – 2 (10 oz.) bag
- Franks red hot sauce – ½ cup
- Ghee – 2.5 tbsp.
- Coconut aminos – 1 tbsp.
- Apple cider vinegar – 1 tsp.

- Garlic powder – ½ tsp.
- Cayenne pepper – ¼ tsp.
- Ranch for dipping
- Chopped green onions or parsley

Method

1. Line a baking sheet with parchment.
2. Preheat the oven to 425F.
3. Place all the sauce ingredients in a saucepan. Heat and mix over medium heat. Once ghee melts, whisk to combine.
4. Combine 1/3 cup buffalo sauce and the cauliflower florets in a bowl. Toss to coat.
5. Place the cauliflower on the sheet pan.
6. Bake 18 to 20 minutes. Tossing once or twice during cooking.
7. Remove from the oven when done.
8. Transfer to a bowl and drizzle with the additional sauce.
9. Top with parsley or green onions and serve with ranch dipping.

Chicken and Sweet Potato Pizza Bites

| Prep time: 20 minutes | Cook time: 15 minutes | Servings: 12 |

Ingredients

- Medium sweet potatoes – 2, sliced into 24 (½ inch) rounds
- Olive or avocado oil – 1 tbsp.
- Cooked chicken breast – 1 lb.
- Green pepper – ¼ cup, diced
- Red onion – ¼ cup, diced
- Canned black olives – ¼ cup, chopped

- Whole30 ranch dressing – ½ cup

For the sauce

- Tomato paste – 1 (6 oz.) can
- Water – 1/3 cup
- Italian seasoning – 2 tsp.
- Garlic powder – 1 ½ tsp.
- Crushed red pepper flakes – ½ tsp.
- Sea salt – ½ tsp.
- Black pepper – ¼ tsp.

Method

1. Preheat the oven to 400F.
2. Place the sweet potato rounds on a baking sheet and coat both sides with oil.
3. Bake for 10 minutes. Then remove from the oven and set aside.
4. Shred the cooked chicken.
5. Add 2 tsp. oil in a pan and heat over medium heat.
6. Add the olives, onions, and peppers. Cook for 1 minute then add the chicken.
7. Cook 2 to 3 minutes on medium heat and turn the heat off.
8. To make the pizza sauce: combine all the ingredients in a pan and heat over medium heat.

9. To assemble: top sweet potato rounds with sauce, then add cooked chicken.

10. Place in the oven and heat until heated through, about 3 to 5 minutes.

11. Drizzle with ranch and serve.

Roasted Brussels Sprouts with Aioli

| Prep time: 10 minutes | Cook time: 35 minutes | Servings: 10 |

Ingredients for Brussels sprouts

- Brussels sprouts – 1 lb. prepared and sliced into half
- Avocado oil – 2 tbsp.
- Sea salt and cracked black pepper

For Aioli

- Mayo – 1/3 cup

- Lemon juice – 2 tsp.
- Garlic – 2 cloves, minced
- Cooked bacon – 2 strips, finely chopped, additional for topping
- Horseradish mustard – 1 tsp.
- Fresh thyme – 1 tsp. plus additional for topping

Method

1. Preheat the oven to 350F.
2. Place Brussels on a sheet pan and drizzle with oil. Season with salt and pepper. Coat well.
3. Roast in the oven until lightly browned, about 30 to 35 minutes. Flip them after every 10 minutes.
4. Meanwhile, in a small bowl, combine the aioli ingredients and mix well. Keep in the refrigerator.
5. Serve roasted Brussels sprouts with aioli.

Buffalo Chicken Sliders

Prep time: 15 minutes	Cook time: 30 minutes	Servings: 4

Ingredients

- Ground chicken – 1 lb.
- Garlic – 1 clove, minced
- Green onions – 2, white and green parts, thinly sliced
- Hot buffalo sauce – 2 to 3 tbsp.
- Almond flour – 2 tbsp.
- Black pepper – ¼ tsp.

- Large sweet potato with skin – 1, sliced into ¼ inch rounds
- Ranch dressing – ¼ cup
- Toppings: avocado slices, sliced onion, leaf lettuce, sliced tomatoes

Method

1. Line a baking sheet with parchment paper.
2. Preheat the oven to 375F.
3. Arrange the potato slices on the baking sheet in a single layer.
4. Bake until tender and lightly browned, about 15 to 20 minutes. Rotate once.
5. In a bowl, combine almond flour, black pepper, buffalo sauce, green onions, garlic, and chicken. Mix well.
6. Preheat grill to about 400F.
7. Make 8 patties with the chicken mixture.
8. Place over hot grill and grill until cooked through, about 5 minutes on each side.

Chicken and Pineapple Kebabs

| Prep time: 25 minutes | Cook time: 15 minutes | Servings: 4 |

Ingredients for the Kebabs

- Chicken breasts – 1 ¼ lb. boneless, skinless
- Fresh pineapple – 2 cups
- Large bell pepper – 1
- Large red onion – ½

For the marinade

- Coconut aminos – ¼ cups
- Water – 1 tbsp.
- Garlic powder – ½ tsp.
- Dried ground ginger – ¼ tsp.
- Toasted sesame oil – 1 tbsp.

Method

1. Cut all the kebab ingredients into 1-inch chunks.
2. In a bowl, combine all the sauce ingredients and whisk. Add chicken and coat well.
3. Preheat the grill to medium-high direct heat.
4. Thread onions, peppers, pineapple, and meat.
5. Brush them with the marinade.
6. Grill until the vegetable is tender and chicken is cooked through. Turning every 5 minutes.
7. Serve.

Crispy Baked Buffalo Wings

| Prep time: 10 minutes | Cook time: 1 hour 10 minutes | Servings: 6 |

Ingredients for wings

- Chicken wings – 3 lb. about 36 pieces
- 2 tsp. cream of tartar and 1 tsp. baking soda, mixed
- Sea salt – 1 tsp.

For the sauce

- Ghee or coconut oil – 1/3 cup
- Frank's red hot sauce – ½ cup
- Organic apple cider vinegar – 1 tbsp.
- Garlic powder – 1 tsp.
- Paprika – ½ tsp.
- Cayenne pepper – 1 pinch
- Sea salt – ½ tsp.

Method

1. Preheat the oven to 250F.
2. Line a baking sheet with foil.
3. Then place a cooling rack on the baking sheet and set aside.
4. In a large bowl, place the chicken wings. Season with sea salt and baking powder. Toss to coat.
5. Arrange the chicken on the cooling rack in a single layer. Keep them separate.
6. Cook in the oven for 30 minutes.
7. Lower the temperature to 425F after 30 minutes of cooking. Then cook for 20 minutes more.
8. Rotate the pan after 20 minutes of cooking and cook until chicken is lightly browned and crispy, about another 20 minutes.
9. Meanwhile, prepare the sauce: combine all the ingredients in a pan and mix over medium heat.

10. Remove the chicken from the oven and place them in a bowl.

11. Coat well with ½ the sauce.

12. Serve with the remaining sauce.

Bacon jalapeno Poppers

| Prep time: 10 minutes | Cook time: 30 minutes | Servings: 20 |

Ingredients

- Jalapenos – 10, prepared and cut in half
- Large avocado – 1
- Cashews - 1 cup, soaked overnight
- Enchilada sauce – ½ cup
- Bacon – 1 (16 oz.) package

Method

1. Preheat the oven to 400F.
2. Place the cashews and sauce in a food processor and mix until smooth.
3. Top each jalapeno half with the cashew mixture and top the mixture with a slice of avocado.
4. Wrap one slice of bacon around each jalapeno.
5. Place a cooling rack on top of a baking sheet.
6. Place the wrapped jalapenos on the cooling rack.
7. Cook in the oven for 30 minutes.
8. Serve.

Chorizo Stuffed Mushrooms

| Prep time: 15 minutes | Cook time: 30 minutes | Servings: 12 |

Ingredients

- No sugar chorizo – 1 lb.
- Ghee – 1 tbsp.
- Medium yellow onion – ½, finely diced
- Red bell pepper – ½, finely diced
- Garlic – 3 cloves, minced

- Button mushrooms – 2 lb. stems removed (keep ½ steams for filling, chopped)
- Fresh spinach – 2 cup, chopped
- Fresh parsley – ¼ cup, chopped

Method

1. Preheat the oven to 350F.
2. Line a baking sheet with parchment paper and set aside.
3. Melt the ghee in a skillet.
4. Add the mushrooms and sauté until they release water.
5. Add bell pepper and onion. Continue to cook and stir for 30 seconds.
6. Remove the skillet from the heat. Add parsley and greens. Stir to mix.
7. Cool slightly, then add chorizo. Mix well.
8. Scoop chorizo mixture into each mushroom.
9. Bake in the oven at 350F until mushrooms are tender and filling is cooked through, about 25 to 30 minutes.
10. Arrange on a serving plate.
11. Top with parsley and serve.

Sausage Stuffed Mushrooms

| Prep time: 15 minutes | Cook time: 25 minutes | Servings: 30 mushrooms |

Ingredients

- Ground sausage – 8 ounce
- Baby Bella or white button mushrooms – 30 to 35, stems removed
- Shredded apples – ½ cup, skinned cored
- Chopped leeks – ¼ cups
- Finely chopped pecans – ¼ cups
- Avocado oil or olive oil – 3 tbsp. divided
- Chopped dried cranberries – 1/3 cup

- Chopped fresh sage – 2 tbsp.
- Eggs – 2, beaten
- Garlic – 1 clove, minced

Method

1. Preheat the oven to 350F.
2. Lightly grease a large baking sheet. Set aside.
3. Heat a skillet and add 2 tbsp. oil.
4. Add sausage and cook for 2 to 3 minutes.
5. Add in pecans, apples, and leeks. Sauté until sausage is cooked completely, about 4 to 5 minutes.
6. Pour mixture into a bowl. Add in the eggs, sage, and cranberries. Mix well.
7. Add and mix the remaining oil with crushed garlic.
8. Brush the caps of each mushroom with garlic-oil mixture and place them inside the baking sheet.
9. Spoon the mixture in each mushroom cap.
10. Place in the oven and bake until the mushrooms are browned, about 25 minutes.

BBQ Muffins with Topping

Prep time: 10 minutes	Cook time: 20 minutes	Servings: 4

Ingredients

- Ground beef – 1 ½ lb.
- Ghee or cooling oil – 2 tsp.

- Small onion – 1, minced
- Garlic – 3 cloves, minced
- Whole30 compliant barbecue sauce – ½ cup
- Dried thyme – 1 tsp.
- Sea salt – ½ tsp.
- Black pepper – ½ tsp.

Topping

- Sweet potato – 2 medium, peeled and cubed
- Coconut oil – 1 tbsp. or ghee
- Sea salt – ¼ tsp.

Method

1. Preheat the oven to 350F.
2. Place the ground beef in a bowl and set aside.
3. Heat oil in a skillet over medium heat. Add onions and sauté until softened. Stirring occasionally.
4. Add garlic and cook until fragrant.
5. Add garlic-onion mixture to the beef. Season with thyme, pepper, sea salt and sauce. Mix with your hands.
6. Divide the mixture and place in 12 wells of a muffin pan.
7. Bake in the oven until meat is no longer pink in the center, about 20 minutes.
8. Meanwhile, steam sweet potatoes for 10 to 12 minutes or until tender.

9. When cooked, mash the potatoes and ghee with a fork.
10. Scoop the mixture onto the meatloaves.
11. Drizzle with barbecue sauce and serve.

Zucchini Turkey Meatballs

| Prep time: 10 minutes | Cook time: 16 minutes | Servings: 4 |

Ingredients

- Ground turkey – 1 lb.
- Shredded zucchini – 1 cup (liquid removed)
- Dried Italian seasoning -1 tsp.
- Garlic powder – ½ tsp.
- Onion powder – ½ tsp.

- Crushed red pepper – ¼ tsp.
- Sea salt – ½ tsp.
- Black pepper – ¼ sp.

Method

1. Preheat the oven to 400F.
2. Cover a cooking sheet with parchment.
3. In a bowl, combine all the ingredients and mix with hands.
4. Make 12 meatballs and place on the baking sheet.
5. Bake until meatballs cooked through, about 16 to 18 minutes.
6. Serve.

Chicken Zucchini Poppers

| Prep time: 15 minutes | Cook time: 20 minutes | Servings: 4 to 5 |

Ingredients

- Ground chicken breast – 1 lb. raw
- Grated zucchini (with peel) – 2 cups, some of the liquid removed
- Green onions – 2 to 3, sliced
- Cilantro – 3 to 4 tbsp. minced
- Garlic – 1 clove, minced
- Salt – 1 tsp.
- Pepper – ½ tsp.
- Cumin – ¾ tsp.

Method

1. Mix together the green onion, zucchini, chicken, cumin, cilantro, garlic, salt, and pepper. Mix well and make meatballs.

2. Preheat the oven to 400F.

3. Line a baking sheet with foil and grease it with oil.

4. Bake at 400F until cooked through, about 15 to 20 minutes.

5. If you want, place under the broiler until browned on top.

6. Serve.

Chapter 4 Salad Recipes

Spicy Tuna Rolls

| Prep time: 35 minutes | Total time: 35 minutes | Servings: 2 |

Ingredients

- o   Sushi grade tuna – ½ pound, diced
- o   Whole30 compliant mayonnaise – 1 tbsp.
- o   Whole30 sriracha – 1 tbsp.
- o   Nori sheets – 4
- o   Unpeeled English cucumber – 1 cup, cut into matchsticks

- Fresh ginger – 1, 3-inch piece (cut into matchsticks)
- Avocado – 1, cut into 16 sliced
- Thinly sliced green onions – ¼ cup
- Black sesame seeds – 1 tbsp.
- Whole30 compliant wasabi
- Coconut aminos

Method

1. Combine the tuna, mayonnaise, and sriracha in a large bowl.
2. Fold each nori sheet lengthwise and crosswise until it breaks easily into 4 pieces to create 16 squares.
3. For each roll, place 1 slice avocado, 2 ginger matchsticks, 2 cucumber matchsticks, 2 sliced green onion, and 1 rounded tbsp. of tuna mixture diagonally at the bottom left corner of a nori square.
4. Sprinkle with some of the sesame seeds. Gently roll into a cone and tuck the pointed end under.
5. Serve the rolls with coconut aminos and wasabi.

Hot Beef and Broccoli Salad

| Prep time: 15 minutes | Cook time: 15 minutes | Servings: 4 |

Ingredients

- Boneless beef sirloin steak – 1 pound
- Salt – ½ tsp.
- Black pepper – ¼ tsp.
- Grated lemon zest – 2 tsp.
- Lemon –garlic dressing – 6 tbsp.
- Broccoli florets – 3 cups
- Orange or red bell pepper – 1 large, sliced
- Baby spinach – 1 package (9 ounces)

- Fresh chives – ¼ cup, snipped

Method

1. Slice the meat into bite size pieces and season with lemon zest, salt, and pepper. Drizzle with 2 tbsp. of dressing and toss to mix.
2. In a large bowl, combine bell pepper, broccoli, and 3 tbsp. of the dressing. Toss to coat.
3. Cook and stir the bell pepper and broccoli in a large skillet for 3 minutes.
4. Return the vegetable to the large bowl.
5. Add the meat to the same skillet. Cook and stir for 1 to 2 minutes or until slightly pink in the center.
6. Add the vegetables and stir to combine.
7. In a large bowl, toss the greens with the remaining 1 tbsp. dressing.
8. Serve the meat and vegetables over the greens.
9. Sprinkle the salad with the snipped chives.

Grilled Steak and Onion Salad

Prep time: 15 minutes	Grill time: 20 minutes	Servings: 4

Ingredients for the steak and onions

- o Flank steak or skirt steak – 1 (16 to 20 ounces)
- o Cumin seeds – 1 tbsp. lightly crushed

- Salt – 1 tsp.
- Black pepper – 1 tsp.
- Large onion – 1
- Extra-virgin olive oil – 2 tbsp.

For the dressing

- Mayonnaise – ¾ cup
- Grated zest and juice of 1 lime
- Whole30 compliant hot sauce – 2 tsp.
- Chopped iceberg lettuce – 8 cups
- Avocados – 2, diced
- Chopped fresh cilantro

Method

1. Preheat a grill to 375F.
2. Grill the steak and onions. Season the steak with salt, pepper and cumin seeds. Cut the onion into ½-inch thick slices and drizzle the steak and onions with olive oil.
3. Grill the steak and onion slices over direct heat. Steak for 15 to 20 minutes for medium (160F) and onion for 5 to 6 minutes. Turning once.
4. Remove from heat and let rest for 5 minutes.
5. Meanwhile, in a small bowl, combine the hot sauce, lime zest, juice, and mayonnaise.

6. Coarsely chop the onions and thinly slice the steak.
7. Place the lettuce in a serving bowl and top with the steak and onions.
8. Drizzle the dressing over the salad.
9. Top with avocado and cilantro.
10. Serve.

BBQ-Pulled-Chicken Lettuce Wraps

| Prep time: 10 minutes | Grill time: 25 minutes | Servings: 4 |

Ingredients

- Boneless, skinless chicken breasts – 1 pound
- Whole30 compliant barbecue sauce – ½ to ¾ cup
- Shredded carrots – 1 cup
- Chopped fresh cilantro – 2 tbsp.
- Fresh lime juice – 2 tbsp.
- Romaine lettuce leaves – 8

Method

1. In a saucepan, add the chicken and enough water to cover. Bring to a boil, then lower the heat. Cover and

simmer for 15 to 20 minutes, or until the chicken is cooked.

2. Transfer the chicken to a cutting board and let cool slightly. Discard the water.

3. Shred the chicken with forks. Return the chicken to the dry pan and stir in the barbecue sauce.

4. Cook for 2 minutes.

5. In a bowl, combine lime juice, cilantro, and carrots. Serve the BBQ chicken and carrot mixture in the lettuce leaves.

Salmon and Potato Salad

| Prep time: 10 minutes | Grill time: 15 minutes | Servings: 4 |

Ingredients

- Baby yellow potatoes – 1 ½ pound, halved
- Avocado oil – 1/3 cup
- Whole30 compliant Dijon mustard – 1 tbsp.
- Fresh lemon juice – 1 tbsp.
- Salt – ½ tsp.
- Black pepper – ½ tsp.
- Salmon – 1 can (6 ounces) drained
- Arugula – 2 cups

- Green onions – 3, sliced
- Snipped fresh chives – 2 tbsp.
- Minced fresh parsley – 1 tbsp.

Method

1. Boil the potatoes for 15 minutes or until tender.
2. In a large bowl, whisk together the lemon juice, mustard, avocado oil, salt, and pepper. Add the parsley, chives, green onions, arugula, salmon and potatoes. Toss to coat.
3. Serve warm.

Curry Chicken Salad

| Prep time: 15 minutes | Total time: 15 minutes | Servings: 3 to 4 |

Ingredients

- Mayonnaise – ½ cup
- Fresh lime juice – 1 tbsp.
- Fresh cilantro – 2 tbsp.
- Whole-30 compliant curry powder – 2 tsp.
- Salt – ¼ tsp.

- Diced cooked chicken – 2 cups
- Medium apple – ½, diced
- Celery stalk – 1, finely diced
- Finely diced red onion – 3 tbsp.
- Dry-roasted cashews – ¼ cup, roughly chopped
- Shredded cabbage, sliced green onions, shredded carrots

Method

1. In a bowl, stir together the curry powder, cilantro, salt, lime juice, and mayonnaise. Add the onion, celery, apple, and chicken. Fold in the cashews.
2. Top the salad with carrots, cabbage, and green onions.
3. Serve.

Tuna, Snow Pea and Broccoli Salad with Dressing

| Prep time: 10 minutes | Grill time: 10 minutes | Servings: 4 |

Ingredients for the dressing

- Grated orange zest – 1 tsp.
- Extra-virgin olive oil – 3 tbsp.
- Rice vinegar – 3 tbsp.
- Toasted sesame oil – 1 tbsp.

For the salad

- Orange – 1, peeled and cut into bite-size pieces
- Broccoli slaw – 1 bag (12 ounces)
- Fresh snow peas – 1 package (8 ounces), trimmed and halved diagonally

- Water-packed wild albacore tuna – 2 (5 ounces each) cans, drained and broken into chunks

Method

1. Make the dressing, in a small bowl; combine the sesame oil, vinegar, olive oil, and orange zest.
2. In another bowl, combine the broccoli slaw, orange pieces, snow peas, and tuna. Drizzle with the dressing and gently toss.
3. Serve.

Shrimp and Mango Salad

| Prep time: 15 minutes | Cook time: 5 minutes | Servings: 2 |

Ingredients for dressing

- Grated lime zest – ½ tsp.
- Fresh lime juice – 2 tbsp.
- Extra-virgin olive oil – ¼ cup
- Chopped fresh cilantro – 1 tbsp.
- Finely chopped seeded jalapeno – 2 tsp.
- Salt – 1/8 tsp.

For the salad

- Extra-virgin olive oil – 1 tbsp.
- Peeled and deveined large shrimp – 8 ounces
- Chili powder – 1 tsp.
- Salt – 1/8 tsp.
- Torn Bibb lettuce leaves – 6 cups
- Medium ripe mango – 1, diced
- Medium ripe avocado – 1, diced

Method

1. To make the dressing, in a bowl, combine the lemon juice and zest. Whisk and drizzle in the olive oil. Stir in the jalapeno, cilantro, and salt. Mix well.
2. To make the salad, in a large skillet, heat the olive oil over medium heat.
3. Add the shrimp, chili powder, and salt. Cook and stir for 5 minutes.
4. Arrange the lettuce on serving plates. Top with shrimp, avocado and mango.
5. Drizzle with dressing and serve.

Pork Greek Salad

| Prep time: 10 minutes | Cook time: 10 minutes | Servings: 4 |

Ingredients for the pork

- Ground pork – 1 pound
- Greek seasoning – 1 tsp.
- Thinly sliced red onion – ½ cup
- Sliced pitted Kalamata olives – ½ cup

For the salad

- Red wine vinegar – 3 tbsp.
- Garlic – 2 cloves, minced
- Greek seasoning – 1 tsp.
- Extra-virgin olive oil – ¼ cup
- Chopped romaine lettuce – 8 cups
- Medium cucumber – 1, chopped

Method

1. In a skillet, cook the pork and Greek seasoning over medium heat for 6 to 8 minutes, or until browned and crispy.
2. Turn off the heat and stir in olives and red onion. Let stand for 2 minutes to soften the onion.
3. Meanwhile, in a small bowl, combine the Greek seasoning, garlic, and vinegar. Whisk in the olive oil until well combined.
4. Arrange the lettuce, cucumber, and pork in the bowls. Drizzle with the dressing and serve.

Beef Salad Wraps

| Prep time: 10 minutes | Total time: 10 minutes | Servings: 2 |

Ingredients for dressing

- Mayonnaise – ¼ cup
- Garlic – 1 clove, minced
- Chopped fresh basil – 1 tbsp.
- Grated lemon zest – ½ tsp.
- Fresh lemon juice – 1 tsp.

For the wraps

- Bibb lettuce leaves – 12 large
- Sliced roast beef – 8 ounces, cut into ½ inch strips

- Avocado – 1 medium, diced
- Halved cherry tomatoes – 1 cup

Method

1. Make the dressing, in a small bowl, stir together the basil, garlic, mayonnaise, and lemon zest and juice.
2. Arrange the lettuce leaves on two serving plates.
3. Divide the tomatoes, avocado and roast beef strips among the leaves.
4. Drizzle with the dressing and serve.

Prosciutto and Shrimp in Red Cabbage Cups

| Prep time: 15 minutes | Cook time: 10 minutes | Servings: 4 |

Ingredients

- Extra-virgin olive oil – 2 tbsp.
- Sliced prosciutto – 2 ounces, chopped
- Large shrimp – 1 pound, peeled and deveined
- Red bell pepper – 1, chopped
- Garlic – 3 cloves, chopped
- Italian seasoning – 2 tsp.

- Salt – ½ tsp.
- Black pepper – ½ tsp.
- Chopped fresh basil – ½ cup
- White wine vinegar – 1 tbsp.
- Bibb lettuce – 1 small head

Method

1. Heat the olive oil in a large skillet over medium heat.
2. Add prosciutto. Cook and stir for 2 to 3 minutes, or until crisp. Transfer the prosciutto to paper towels to drain.
3. Increase the heat to medium-high. Add the bell pepper and shrimp. Cook and stir occasionally for 2 minutes or until the pepper is softened and the shrimp are almost opaque.
4. Add Italian seasoning, salt, black pepper, and garlic. Cook and stir for 2 to 3 more minutes.
5. Remove from the heat and stir in the basil and vinegar.
6. Separate the leaves from the cabbage and arrange on a platter.
7. Spoon the shrimp filling into the leaves, top with prosciutto and serve.

Spicy Chicken with Salad

| Prep time: 15 minutes | Cook time: 10 minutes | Servings: 2 |

Ingredients for the chicken

- Skinless, boneless chicken breasts – 2 (6 ounces each) flatten to a ¼ inch thickness
- Red pepper flakes – 1 tsp.
- Garlic powder – ½ tsp.
- Salt – ½ tsp.
- Black pepper – ½ tsp.
- Extra-virgin olive oil – 2 tbsp.

For the salad

- Baby spinach – 4 cups
- Chopped seedless watermelon – 2 cups
- Finely chopped shallot – ¼ cup
- Extra-virgin olive oil – 3 tbsp.
- Red wine vinegar – 2 tbsp.
- Salt – ½ tsp.
- Black pepper – ½ tsp.
- Roasted salted pistachios – 1/3 cup, chopped

Method

1. Combine the pepper flakes, garlic powder, salt, and pepper in a small bowl. Sprinkle the seasoning over the chicken.
2. Heat the olive oil in a skillet over medium heat.
3. Add the chicken and cook for 8 minutes or until cooked through. Turning once.
4. Place the chicken on a cutting board and rest for 5 minutes. Then thinly slice the chicken.
5. Make the salad; combine the shallot, watermelon, and spinach in a large bowl. Drizzle with the vinegar and olive oil. Sprinkle with the salt and black pepper.
6. Toss the salad to coat with the dressing.
7. Arrange the salad and serve.

Pork Radicchio Wraps

| Prep time: 15 minutes | Grill time: 10 minutes | Servings: 2 |

Ingredients

- Fennel bulb – 1 small,
- Extra-virgin olive oil – 1 tbsp.
- Ground pork – 8 ounces
- Small apple – 1, diced
- Dried sage – 1 tsp. crushed
- Salt – ¼ tsp.
- Finely chopped unsulfured dried apricots – 2 tbsp.
- Mayonnaise – 2 tbsp.

- Cider vinegar – 1 tbsp.
- Bibb lettuce or cabbage leaves – 8 medium
- Toasted walnuts – ¼ cup, chopped

Method

1. Trim the fennel bulb, reserve the fronds. Remove the core and chop the bulb.
2. Heat the olive oil in a skillet over medium heat.
3. Add the pork and chopped fennel. Cook and stir for 3 to 4 minutes or until the pork is almost cooked through.
4. Add the sage, apple, and salt. Cook and stir for 2 to 3 minutes more, or until the pork is no longer pink and apple is crisp-tender.
5. Stir in the apricots and remove from the heat.
6. In a small bowl, whisk together the vinegar and mayonnaise.
7. Add the pork mixture and stir until combined.
8. Place the lettuce leaves on a serving plate.
9. Spoon the pork filling and sprinkle with walnuts.
10. Sprinkle with fronds and serve.

Meatball Salad

| Prep time: 15 minutes | Bake time: 20 minutes | Servings: 2 |

Ingredients for the meatballs

- Large egg – 1
- Almond flour – 1/3 cup
- Garlic – 3 cloves, minced
- Dried oregano – 1 tsp. crushed
- Salt – ½ tsp.
- Black pepper – ¼ tsp.
- Ground turkey – 8 ounces

For the salad

- Avocado – ½, sliced
- Coconut milk or flax milk – ¼ cup, unsweetened

- Fresh lemon juice – 1 to 2 tbsp.
- Garlic – 1 clove, minced
- Salt – ¼ tsp.
- Black pepper – 1/8 tsp.
- Chopped fresh mint – 2 tbsp.
- Hearts of romaine – 1 bag (9 ounces)
- English cucumber – ½, sliced and quartered
- Drained roasted red pepper – 2/3 cup, patted dry and chopped

Method

1. Preheat the oven to 400F. Line a baking sheet with parchment paper.
2. Lightly whisk the egg in a bowl. Stir in the black pepper, salt, oregano, garlic, and almond flour.
3. Add the ground turkey and mix.
4. Make 8 meatballs and place on the pan.
5. Bake until the internal temperature is 18 to 20 minutes.
6. Meanwhile, in a blender combine the lemon juice, garlic, salt, black pepper, flax milk, and avocado. Blend until smooth.
7. Transfer to a bowl and stir in the mint.
8. Arrange the salad with meatballs and serve.

Fruity Chicken Salad

| Prep time: 10 minutes | Total time: 10 minutes | Servings: 2 |

Ingredients for the dressing

- Fresh orange juice – 2 tbsp.
- White wine vinegar – 1 tbsp.
- Extra-virgin olive oil – ¼ cup
- Salt – 1/8 tsp.
- Black pepper – 1/8 tsp.

For the salad

- Medium orange – 1, peeled and white pith removed
- Chopped romaine lettuce – 6 cups
- Coarsely chopped cooked chicken – 1 ½ cups
- Pomegranate seeds – ¼ cup

- Coarsely chopped roasted cashews – ¼ cup
- Green onions – 2, sliced

Method

1. To make the dressing, in a small bowl, whisk together the vinegar, olive oil, salt, pepper, and orange juice.
2. Make the salad, divide the orange into segments. Arrange the lettuce in the serving bowls.
3. Top with the orange segments, chicken, pomegranate seeds, green onions, and cashews.
4. Drizzle with the dressing and serve.

Chapter 5 Bowl Meals

Scallop Noodle Bowls

| Prep time: 5 minutes | Cook time: 10 minutes | Servings: 2 |

Ingredients

- Small sea scallops – 1 pound
- Smoked paprika – 1 tbsp.
- Salt – ½ tsp.
- Ghee or extra-virgin olive oil – 2 tbsp.
- Garlic – 2 cloves, sliced
- Cherry tomatoes – 2 cups
- Chicken broth – 1 cup
- Fresh lemon juice – 1 tbsp.
- Zucchini – 2, medium, spiralized
- Chopped fresh parsley – 1 tbsp.

Method

1. Rinse the scallops and pat dry with a paper towel.
2. Season with paprika and salt.
3. In a large skillet, heat 1 tbsp. of butter over medium heat.
4. Add the scallops and sear each side for 1 minute.
5. Remove from the skillet and keep warm.
6. Add the tomatoes and garlic to the skillet. Cook and stir over medium heat for 3 minutes, or until the tomatoes are lightly charred and start to burst.
7. Add the scallops, lemon juice, and broth and cook for 2 minutes or until the scallops are just cooked.
8. Meanwhile, in a large skillet, cook the zucchini noodles in the remaining 1 tbsp. butter for 1 to 2 minutes, or until just tender.
9. Serve the tomatoes, scallops, and broth over the noodles in bowls.
10. Top with fresh parsley and serve.

Shrimp and Zucchini Noodles Soup

| Prep time: 10 minutes | Cook time: 20 minutes | Servings: 4 |

Ingredients

- Extra-virgin olive oil – 1 tbsp.
- Large onion – 1, chopped
- Jalapenos – 2, large, seeded and finely chopped
- Kosher salt – ¼ tsp.
- Tomato paste – ¼ cup
- Mexican seasoning or chili powder – 1 tbsp.
- Chicken broth – 5 cups
- Small shrimp – 1 pound, peeled and deveined
- Zucchini – 2 small, spiralized
- Fresh cilantro – 1 cup, chopped
- Chopped avocado

- Lime wedges

Method

1. Heat the olive oil in a 4-quart Dutch oven over medium heat. Add the jalapenos, onion, and salt. Cook and stir for 6 to 8 minutes or until softened.

2. Stir in the Mexican seasoning and tomato paste. Cook and stir for 1 minute. Add broth and bring to a boil.

3. Stir in the zucchini noodles and shrimp. Cook for 5 minutes or until shrimp is opaque.

4. Stir in the chopped cilantro.

5. Serve the soup with lime wedges and chopped avocado.

Steak and Mushroom Noodle Bowls

| Prep time: 15 minutes | Cook time: 20 minutes | Servings: 6 |

Ingredients

- Beef stir-fry strips – 1 ½ pound
- Italian seasoning – 2 tsp.
- Salt – ½ tsp.
- Black pepper – ½ tsp.
- Olive oil – 2 tbsp.
- Frozen bell pepper and onion blend – 1 bag (14 ounces)
- Beef broth – 4 cups
- Diced tomatoes with garlic and onion – 1 can (14.5 ounces)

- Portobello mushrooms – 2, gills removed, halved and sliced
- Rutabaga – 1 medium, diced
- Fresh basil leaves – 1 cup

Method

1. Season the meat with the salt, pepper and Italian seasoning.
2. In a large pot, heat 1 tbsp. of the olive oil over medium heat.
3. Add half of the meat. Cook and stir for 2 to 3 minutes or until browned, but pink in the center. Transfer the meat to a bowl.
4. Add the remaining 1 tbsp. olive oil and meat in the pot. Cook as before and transfer the meat to the bowl.
5. Add the onion and bell pepper blend to the pot.
6. Cook over medium heat for 3 to 4 minutes or until tender. Stirring occasionally.
7. Add the tomatoes and broth and bring to a boil.
8. Add the rutabaga and mushrooms and bring to a low boil.
9. Cook for 6 to 7 minutes or until mushrooms and rutabaga are just tender.
10. Return the meat to the pot, stir in the basil and serve.

Chicken Zoodle Soup

| Prep time: 10 minutes | Cook time: 20 minutes | Servings: 2 |

Ingredients

- Coconut oil – 1 tbsp.
- Boneless, skinless chicken breast – 1 large (8 ounces)
- Chicken broth – 2 cups
- Minced fresh ginger – 1 tbsp.
- Fish sauce – 2 tsp.
- Red pepper flakes – 1/8 to ¼ tsp.
- Zucchini – 1 small, spiralized – 1 ½ cups
- Carrot – 1 medium, ½ cup, shredded

- Sliced green onions – ¼ cup
- Chopped fresh cilantro – 2 tbsp. plus more for garnish
- Fresh bean sprouts – ½ cup
- Chopped fresh mint – 2 tbsp.

Method

1. Heat the coconut oil in a large saucepan over medium heat.
2. Add the chicken. Cook and stir for 6 to 8 minutes or until well browned on both sides. Remove the pan from the heat.
3. Add the fish sauce, pepper flakes, ginger, and broth.
4. Return to the heat and bring to a boil.
5. Reduce the heat and simmer for 5 to 6 minutes or until the internal temperature of the chicken reaches 165F.
6. Transfer the chicken to a cutting board to cool slightly.
7. Add the carrots and zucchini noodles to the hot broth.
8. Cover over medium heat for 1 to 2 minutes or until vegetables are crisp-tender.
9. Shred the chicken with forks.
10. Add the chicken back to the pan and gently stir in the cilantro and green onions.
11. Top servings with mint, bean sprouts, and more cilantro.

Creamy Broccoli-Kale Soup

| Prep time: 15 minutes | Cook time: 15 minutes | Servings: 4 |

Ingredients

- Extra-virgin olive oil – 1 tbsp.
- Leeks – 2, white parts only, cut into 1-inch pieces
- Garlic – 2 cloves, minced
- Broccoli – 1 pound, trimmed and chopped
- Kale – 1 bunch, stalks removed and leaves chopped
- Salt – ½ tsp.
- Red pepper flakes – 1/8 tsp.
- Chicken broth – 5 cups
- Coconut milk – 1 can (13.5 ounces)

Method

1. Heat the olive oil in a large pot over medium heat.
2. Add the garlic and leeks. Cook and stir for 3 to 5 minutes or until softened.
3. Stir in the broth, pepper flakes, salt, kale, and broccoli. Bring to a boil.
4. Lower the heat to low. Cover and simmer for 10 minutes or until broccoli is tender. Stirring occasionally.
5. Add 1 cup of coconut milk and cook for 1 minute or heated through.
6. Use a hand blender to blend the soup directly in the pot.
7. Top servings with coconut milk and serve.

Asparagus, Prosciutto Soup

| Prep time: 25 minutes | Cook time: 25 minutes | Servings: 4 |

Ingredients

- Coconut oil – 2 tbsp.
- Onion – 1 medium, chopped
- Asparagus – 2 bunches, tips and stalks (stalks cut into 1-inch pieces)
- Chicken broth – 5 cups
- Chopped fresh tarragon – 1 tbsp.
- Coconut milk – ½ cup
- Fresh lemon juice – 2 tbsp.
- Salt – ½ tsp.

- Black pepper – ¼ tsp.
- Prosciutto – 2 slices, rolled up and cut into ribbons

Method

1. In a large pot, heat the coconut oil over medium heat.
2. Add the onion and cook for 5 minutes or until tender. Stirring occasionally.
3. Add the asparagus stalk pieces, tarragon, and broth to the onion and bring to a boil.
4. Lower the heat and cook for 15 minutes.
5. Place the asparagus tips in a metal steamer and lower into the broth mixture.
6. Cook, uncovered for 4 minutes or until just tender.
7. Carefully remove the strainer and run the tips under the cold water. Set aside.
8. Remove the pot from the heat and stir in the lemon juice and coconut milk.
9. Use a hand blender to blend the soup directly in the pot.
10. Season with salt and pepper.
11. Top servings with asparagus tips and prosciutto ribbons.

Southwest Chicken Noodle Bowl

| Prep time: 15 minutes | Cook time: 15 minutes | Servings: 4 |

Ingredients

- Boneless, skinless chicken breast halves – 1 pound, thinly sliced
- Southwest seasoning – 1 tbsp.
- Extra-virgin olive oil – 2 tbsp.
- Chicken broth – 4 cups
- Red and/or yellow bell pepper – 1 large, chopped
- Green onions – 4, trimmed and cut into 1-inch pieces
- Russet potato – 1 medium, peeled and spiralized
- Fresh salsa – 1 cup
- Fresh lemon juice – 2 tbsp.

Method

1. Season the chicken with Southwest seasoning. Rub well.
2. In a skillet, heat 1 tbsp. olive oil over medium heat.
3. Add half of the chicken and cook for 2 minutes, or until no longer pink on the outside. Stirring occasionally.
4. Transfer the chicken on a plate. Repeat with the remaining olive oil and chicken. Then return all the chicken to the skillet.
5. Add the broth and bring to a boil.
6. Stir in the potato noodles, green onions, and bell peppers. Return to a boil.
7. Reduce the heat and simmer for 3 minutes, or until the chicken is cooked through and the vegetables are tender. Stir occasionally.
8. Gently stir in the lemon juice and salsa and serve.

Turkey and Sweet Potato Soup

| Prep time: 10 minutes | Cook time: 20 minutes | Servings: 4 |

Ingredients

- Ground turkey – 1 ½ pound
- Fennel seeds – 2 tsp. crushed
- Ground paprika – 2 tsp.
- Garlic – 4 cloves, minced
- Extra-virgin olive oil – 1 tbsp.
- Chicken broth – 4 cups
- Frozen fire roasted sweet potatoes – 1 package (16 ounces)
- Fire roasted tomatoes with garlic – 1 can (15 ounces)
- Italian seasoning – 2 tsp.

- Chopped fresh basil – ½ cup

Method

1. In a bowl, combine the garlic, paprika, fennel seeds, and turkey. Mix well.
2. In a large pot, heat the olive oil over medium heat.
3. Add the turkey. Cook and stir for 8 to 10 minutes or until lightly browned.
4. Add the Italian seasoning, tomatoes, sweet potatoes, and broth and bring to a boil.
5. Reduce the heat and simmer for 10 minutes or until sweet potatoes are tender. Stirring occasionally.
6. Stir in the basil and serve.

Butternut Squash and Apple Soup

| Prep time: 5 minutes | Cook time: 25 minutes | Servings: 4 |

Ingredients

- Ghee or coconut oil – 2 tbsp.
- Yellow onions – 2 medium, coarsely chopped
- Frozen diced butternut squash – 2 bags (10 ounces each)
- Medium apples – 2, roughly chopped
- Minced fresh ginger – 2 tbsp.
- Ground cardamom – 1 tsp.
- Salt -1 tsp.
- Black pepper – ½ tsp.
- Chicken broth – 4 cups
- Coconut milk – 2/3 cup

- Snipped fresh chives – 2 tbsp.

Method
1. Heat the ghee in a large saucepan over medium heat.
2. Add the onion. Cook and stir for 10 to 12 minutes, or until softened.
3. Add the apples and squash. Cook and stir for 8 to 10 minutes, or until browned and tender.
4. Stir in the salt, pepper, cardamom, and ginger.
5. Add the broth, raise the heat and bring to a boil.
6. Lower the heat and stir in the coconut milk.
7. Use a hand blender to blend the soup in the pot.
8. Top each serving with snipped chives and serve.

Mexican Chicken Soup

| Prep time: 10 minutes | Cook time: 20 minutes | Servings: 4 |

Ingredients

- Extra-virgin olive oil – 1 tbsp.
- Chopped onion – ½ cup
- Medium Poblano pepper – 1, seeded and chopped
- Medium yellow or red bell pepper – 1, chopped
- Garlic- 2 cloves, minced
- Salt – ½ tsp.
- Chicken broth – 4 cups
- Fire-roasted diced tomatoes – 1 can (14.5 ounces), undrained
- Chili powder – 2 tsp.
- Shredded cooked chicken – 3 cups

- Fresh cilantro, chopped
- Avocado – 1, halved, and sliced
- Lime wedges

Method

1. Heat the olive oil in a large pot over medium heat.
2. Add the garlic, onion, poblano, bell pepper and salt. Cook and stir for 3 to 5 minutes or until the vegetables are crisp-tender.
3. Stir in the chili powder, tomatoes, and broth and bring to a boil. Lower the heat and simmer for 10 minutes.
4. Add chicken and cook for 1 minute, or until heat through.
5. Serve the soup with avocado, cilantro and lime wedges.

Creamy Leek, Turnip Soup with Bacon

| Prep time: 10 minutes | Cook time: 35 minutes | Servings: 4 |

Ingredients

- Whole30 compliant bacon – 4 slices, diced
- Leeks – 2, white parts only, cut into 1-inch pieces
- Turnips – 2, peeled and chopped
- Zucchini – 1 medium, ends removed and diced
- Coconut milk – 1 can (14.5 ounces)
- Chicken broth – 1 cup
- Garlic powder – 1 tsp.
- Onion powder – 1 tsp.
- Dried rosemary – 1 tsp.
- Salt – 1 tsp.
- Green onions – 2, minced

Method

1. Cook the bacon in a pot over medium heat for 3 minutes or until crisp. Remove and drain on paper towels. Reserve the drippings in the pot.

2. Lower the heat to medium.

3. Add the leeks. Cook and stir for 3 minutes or until softened.

4. Add the zucchini and turnips. Cook and stir for 5 minutes or until tender.

5. Stir in the rosemary, salt, onion powder, garlic powder, broth, and coconut milk. Simmer the soup, covered for 20 minutes.

6. Use a hand blender to blend the soup in the pot.

7. Top servings with green onions and bacon. Serve.

Spicy Sausage and Spinach Soup

| Prep time: 10 minutes | Cook time: 30 minutes | Servings: 4 |

Ingredients

- Spicy ground pork sausage – 1 pound
- Extra-virgin olive oil – 1 tbsp.
- Cauliflower florets – 4 cups
- Medium onion – 1, chopped
- Celery – 3 stalks, chopped
- Fennel bulb – 1, trimmed, cored and chopped
- Garlic – 2 cloves, chopped
- Chicken broth – 5 cups
- Paprika – ¼ tsp.
- Black pepper – ½ tsp.
- Fresh baby spinach leaves – 5 ounces

Method

1. Brown the sausage over medium heat in a large pot. Transfer the sausage and drain on paper towels. Drain off any fat in the skillet.

2. Heat the olive oil in the same pot over medium heat.

3. Add garlic, fennel, celery, onion, and cauliflower. Cook for 5 to 6 minutes. Stir occasionally.

4. Stir in the broth and bring to a boil. Lower the heat and simmer for 15 minutes.

5. Use a hand blender to blend the soup in the pot. Return the soup to the pot and add the black pepper and paprika.

6. Just before serving, stir the spinach and sausage into the soup and serve.

Carrot-Noodle and Pork Bowls

| Prep time: 15 minutes | Cook time: 20 minutes | Servings: 4 |

Ingredients for the pork

- Ground pork – 1 pound
- Toasted sesame oil – 2 tsp.
- Green onions – 2, sliced
- Minced fresh ginger – 2 tsp.
- Garlic – 2 cloves, minced
- Red pepper flakes – 1/8 tsp.
- Coconut aminos – 2 tbsp.

For the carrot noodles

- Carrots – 4 large, peeled and cut into noodles
- Butter or ghee – 1 tbsp.

- Salt – 1/8 tsp.
- Chopped fresh cilantro
- Limed wedges

Method

1. Make the pork: cook the pork in a skillet over medium heat for 10 minutes or until browned. Break up any big chunks. Transfer to a bowl. Drain any fat from the skillet.
2. Heat the sesame oil in the same skillet over medium heat.
3. Add the garlic, pepper flakes, ginger, green onions. Cook and stir for 1 to 2 minutes or until fragrant.
4. Stir in the coconut aminos and pork and cook for 1 minute.
5. Heat the butter in a large skillet over medium heat.
6. Add the carrot noodles, salt and cook for 3 to 4 minutes, or until just tender. Stirring occasionally.
7. Serve the pork mixture on top of the carrot noodles.
8. Top with cilantro and serve with lime wedges.

Gazpacho Noodle Soup

| Prep time: 5 minutes | Total time: 2 hours 5 minutes | Servings: 4 |

Ingredients

- Very small cooked peeled deveined shrimp – 1 package (16 ounces)
- Zucchini – 2 small, spiralized and long noodles snipped
- Tomato juice – 4 cups
- Fresh medium-hot salsa – 1 ½ cups
- Fresh lemon juice – ¼ cup
- Chopped fresh parsley or basil – ¼ cup
- Sliced almonds – 1/3 cup, toasted

Method

1. In a bowl, stir together the lemon juice, salsa, tomato juice, zucchini, shrimp and half of the parsley.
2. Cover and chill for 2 to 24 hours.
3. Top servings with remaining parsley and almonds.

> **Comment [C]:** Please make sure if this correct? 2 to 24 doesn't make sense. I think it should be 22 to 24. But please make sure.

Fish Stew

| Prep time: 15 minutes | Cook time: 10 minutes | Servings: 4 |

Ingredients

- Extra-virgin olive oil – 2 tbsp.
- Medium fennel bulbs – 2, trimmed, cored and chopped
- Medium red bell pepper – 1, chopped
- Garlic – 4 cloves, chopped
- Seafood seasoning – 2 tsp.
- Chicken broth – 4 cups

- Diced tomatoes – 1 can (15 ounces), undrained
- Cod or other white fish fillets – 1 pound, cut into – 1-inch pieces
- Grated zest and juice of 1 tangerine
- Chopped fresh parsley – ½ cup

Method

1. Heat the olive oil in a large pot over medium heat.
2. Add the bell pepper and fennel. Cook for 5 minutes, or until tender. Stirring occasionally.
3. Add the seafood seasoning and garlic and cook for and stir for 1 minute.
4. Add the tomatoes and broth and bring to a boil.
5. Add the cod, lower the heat and simmer for 3 minutes.
6. Remove from the heat.
7. Stir in the juice and zest, and parsley.
8. Serve.

Chapter 6 Main Dishes

Tuna Avocado Salsa

| Prep time: 15 minutes | Cook time: 5 minutes | Servings: 2 |

Ingredients for the salsa

- Mango – 1, diced
- Tomato – 1 medium, diced
- Green onions – 2, minced
- Avocado – 1, diced
- Fresh cilantro – ¼ cup chopped
- Jalapeno – ½, seeded and minced
- Juice of 1 lime
- Salt – 1/8 tsp.
- Black pepper – 1/8 tsp.

For the tuna

- Ahi Tuna Steaks – 2 (4 to 6 ounces each) 1 inch thick
- Avocado oil
- Black sesame seeds – 1 tsp.
- White sesame seeds – 1 tsp.
- Salt – ¼ tsp.
- Black pepper – ¼ tsp.

Method

1. To make the salsa: in a bowl, combine all the salsa ingredients and toss to mix.
2. Brush both sides of the tuna with a small amount of avocado oil. Then season both sides with the black pepper, salt, and sesame seeds.
3. Heat a skillet over medium heat.
4. Add the tuna and sear for 2 minutes on one side. Then flip and sear the other side until browned and crispy, about 2 minutes more.
5. Serve the salsa with tuna steaks.

Shrimp and Asparagus Dinner Omelets

| Prep time: 10 minutes | Cook time: 15 minutes | Servings: 2 |

Ingredients for the filling

- Extra-virgin olive oil, ghee or butter – 1 tsp.
- Asparagus – ¼ pound, prepared and cut into 1-inch pieces
- Cooked, peeled and deveined medium shrimp – 6 ounces, chopped
- Quartered grape tomatoes – ½ cup

For the omelets

- Eggs – 5 large
- Pinch of salt

- Pinch of black pepper
- Butter – 2 tsp.
- Pesto – 2 tbsp.

Method

1. Make the filling: heat the butter in a skillet over medium heat.
2. Add the asparagus. Cook and stir for 3 minutes or until crisp-tender.
3. Stir in tomatoes and shrimp and heat through for 1 to 2 minutes. Transfer the filling to a bowl and cover with the foil to keep warm.
4. Make the omelets: in a bowl, whisk together the eggs, 2 tbsp. water, salt, and pepper.
5. In the same skillet, heat 1 tsp. of the butter and add half of the egg mixture.
6. Cook for 30 to 60 seconds or until the eggs are set.
7. Spoon 1 tbsp. of the pesto over the omelet.
8. Spoon half of the filling over one side of the omelet. Fold the opposite side over the filling.
9. Transfer to a plate and keep warm.
10. Repeat and serve.

Pork Chops with Onions and Potatoes

| Prep time: 20 minutes | Cook time: 10 minutes | Servings: 2 |

Ingredients

- Extra-virgin olive oil – 3 tbsp.
- Whole-grain mustard – 1 tbsp.
- Garlic – 2 cloves, minced
- Chopped fresh rosemary – 1 tsp.
- Salt – ¼ tsp.
- Black pepper – ¼ tsp.
- Small red potatoes – 8, quartered
- Small red onion – 1, cut into 8 wedges
- Pork chops – 2, bone in, cut ½ inch thick

Method

1. In a small bowl, stir together 1 tbsp. olive oil, pepper, salt, rosemary, garlic, and mustard.

2. In another bowl, toss the onion and potatoes with half of the mustard mixture. Brush the remaining mustard mixture on both sides on the chops.

3. Heat 1 tbsp. olive oil in a large skillet over medium heat.

4. Add the chops and cook for 2 minutes, or until browned, turning once. Transfer the chops to a plate and cover to keep warm.

5. Heat the remaining 1 tbsp. olive oil in the same skillet over medium heat.

6. Add the potatoes and onion and cook for 5 minutes, or until browned. Stirring occasionally.

7. Arrange the chops in with the onions and potatoes.

8. Transfer the skillet to the oven and bake for 10 to 15 minutes, or until the internal temperature of the chops is 145F and potatoes are tender.

Orange Chicken with Cauliflower Rice

| Prep time: 15 minutes | Cook time: 10 minutes | Servings: 4 |

Ingredients

- Grated orange zest – 1 tsp.
- Fresh orange juice – ¾ cup
- Coconut aminos – 1 tbsp.
- Rice vinegar – 1 tsp.
- Garlic – 2 cloves, minced
- Minced fresh ginger – 1 tsp.
- Salt – ¼ tsp.
- Tapioca flour – 1 tsp.
- Ghee or butter – 1 tbsp.
- Boneless, skinless chicken breasts – 1 ½ pound, cut into – 1-inch pieces

- Fresh broccoli, carrots, snow peas stir-fry vegetables – 1 bag (12 ounces)
- Cauliflower crumbles – 1 package (16 ounces)
- Green onions – 2, sliced

Method

1. In a small bowl, mix together the ginger, salt, garlic, rice vinegar, coconut aminos, and the orange zest and juice.
2. In another bowl, whisk together the tapioca flour and 2 tsp. cold water until smooth.
3. Heat the butter in a large skillet over medium heat. Add the chicken. Cook and stir for 5 to 6 minutes, or until fully cooked. Transfer the chicken to a plate and keep warm.
4. Stir the orange juice mixture into the same skillet and bring to a boil. Stir over medium-high heat. Whisk in the tapioca flour mixture until smooth.
5. Add the stir-fry vegetables. Cook and stir for 4 to 6 minutes, or until the vegetables are crisp-tender.
6. Stir in the chicken and heat through for 1 minute.
7. Meanwhile, prepare the cauliflower crumbles according to the package directions.
8. Spoon the vegetables and chicken over the cauliflower, sprinkle with green onions and serve.

Chicken Skillet with Sweet Potato Noodles

| Prep time: 15 minutes | Cook time: 10 minutes | Servings: 4 |

Ingredients

- Boneless, skinless chicken breasts – 1 ¼ to 1 ½ pound (flatten to ½ inch thickness)
- Smoked paprika – 1 ½ tsp.
- Salt – 1 tsp.
- Ground cinnamon – ¾ tsp.
- Extra-virgin olive oil – 2 tbsp.
- Medium shallots – 3, sliced
- Large sweet potato – 1, peeled and spiralized
- Diced tomatoes – 1 can (14.5 ounces), undrained

- Unsweetened dates – ½ cup, chopped
- Fresh orange juice – ¼ cup
- Toasted almonds, sliced
- Finely chopped fresh parsley

Method

1. Sprinkle chicken with salt, cinnamon, and paprika.
2. Heat the olive oil in a skillet over medium heat.
3. Add the chicken and shallots. Cook for 2 to 4 minutes or until the chicken is lightly browned but not cooked through, turning once.
4. Transfer the chicken to a plate and cover with foil to keep warm.
5. Add the orange juice, dates, tomatoes and sweet potatoes noodles to the skillet with the shallots. Stir to mix.
6. Return the chicken to the skillet.
7. Bring to a boil over medium heat. Cover and lower the heat to low.
8. Cook for 6 to 8 minutes or until chicken is no longer pink and sweet potato noodles are just tender.
9. Serve with parsley and sliced almonds.

Garlic Shrimp with Veggies

| Prep time: 10 minutes | Cook time: 15 minutes | Servings: 4 |

Ingredients

- Olive oil – 1 tbsp.
- Zucchini – 1 medium trimmed, halved lengthwise, and cut into half-moons
- Red bell pepper – 1 medium, cut into thin strips
- Extra-large shrimp – 1 pound, peeled and deveined
- Garlic – 3 cloves, minced
- Butter or ghee – ¼ cup
- Fresh lemon juice – ¼ cup
- Salt – ½ tsp.
- Black pepper – ¼ tsp.
- Cauliflower crumbles – 1 package (16 ounces)

- Chopped fresh parsley – ¼ cup

Method

1. Heat the olive oil in a large skillet over medium heat.
2. Add pepper strips and zucchini. Cook and stir for 3 minutes.
3. Add garlic and shrimp, cook for 5 to 6 minutes or until the shrimp are opaque. Turning once. Transfer the shrimp mixture to a bowl and cover to keep warm.
4. To make the sauce, melt the butter in a skillet over medium heat. Add the black pepper, salt, and lemon juice. Bring to a boil and whisk until smooth.
5. Meanwhile, cook the cauliflower crumbles according to the package directions.
6. Spoon the vegetables and shrimp over the cauliflower. Drizzle with lemon sauce, sprinkle with parsley and serve.

Beef Skillet

Prep time: 20 minutes	Cook time: 10 minutes	Servings: 4

Ingredients

- Ground beef – 1 pound
- Extra-virgin olive oil – 1 tbsp.
- Small red onion – 1, chopped
- Small red bell pepper – 1, chopped
- Small yellow bell pepper – 1, chopped
- Garlic – 2 cloves, minced
- Salt – ½ tsp.

- Chili powder – 2 tsp.
- Ground cumin – ¼ tsp.
- Cayenne pepper – 1/8 tsp.
- Fresh lime juice – 1 tbsp.
- Chopped fresh cilantro – 2 tbsp.
- Cauliflower crumbles – 1 package (16 ounces)
- Diced avocado or tomato
- Lime wedges

Method

1. Cook the beef over medium heat in a large skillet for 5 minutes or until browned. Break up large chunks with a spoon. Drain off any fat and transfer the beef to a bowl.
2. Heat the olive oil in the same skillet over medium heat.
3. Add the garlic, salt, bell peppers and onion. Cook for 4 to 6 minutes, or until the vegetables are crisp-tender. Stirring occasionally.
4. Stir in the cayenne, cumin, chili powder, and beef and heat through for 1 minute.
5. Stir in the lime juice. Remove the skillet from the heat and stir in the cilantro.
6. Meanwhile, prepare the cauliflower crumbles according to the package directions.
7. Spoon the vegetables and beef over the cauliflower and top with tomato or avocado.
8. Serve with lime wedges.

Turkey and Squash Chili

| Prep time: 5 minutes | Cook time: 20 minutes | Servings: 4 |

Ingredients

- Extra-virgin olive oil – 1 tbsp.
- Ground turkey – 1 pound
- Garlic – 2 cloves, minced
- Fresh or frozen diced carrots, celery or onion blend – 1 package (14 ounces)
- Chili powder – 2 tbsp.
- Ground cumin – 2 tsp.
- Salt – ½ tsp.
- Chopped butternut squash – 1 package (12 ounces)
- Fire-roasted diced tomatoes, undrained – 1 can (28 ounces)

- For topping: sliced green onions, chopped fresh cilantro, guacamole, chopped jalapeno, and/or lime wedges

Method

1. Heat the olive oil in a large skillet over medium heat.
2. Add the garlic and turkey. Cook and break up the large chunks for 5 minutes, or until turkey is browned.
3. Add the cumin, salt, chili powder and carrot mixture. Cook for 5 minutes, or until the vegetables are tender. Stirring occasionally.
4. Add the tomatoes and squash and bring to a boil. Lower the heat and simmer for 10 to 12 minutes, or until the squash is tender. Stirring occasionally.
5. Serve with toppings.

Red Curry Shrimp Skillet

| Prep time: 20 minutes | Cook time: 15 minutes | Servings: 4 |

Ingredients

- Coconut oil – 1 tbsp.
- Small onion – 1, chopped
- Garlic – 2 cloves, minced
- Minced fresh ginger – 2 tsp.
- Coconut milk – 1 can (14 ounces)
- Thai red curry paste – 2 tbsp.
- Coconut aminos – 1 tbsp.
- Peeled and deveined large shrimp – 1 pound
- Fresh baby spinach – 4 cups
- Fresh lime juice – 1 tbsp. plus more for serving
- Cauliflower crumbles – 1 package (16 ounces)

- Torn fresh basil
- Lime wedges

Method

1. Heat the olive oil over medium heat in a skillet.
2. Add the onion, cook for 3 to 4 minutes. Stirring occasionally.
3. Add the ginger and garlic and cook and stir for 1 minute, or until fragrant.
4. Sir in the coconut aminos, curry paste and coconut milk.
5. Bring to a boil, then lower the heat and simmer for 5 minutes.
6. Add the shrimp and cook for 5 minutes or until opaque. Stirring occasionally.
7. Remove from the heat and stir in the lime juice and spinach.
8. Meanwhile, prepare the cauliflower crumbles according to the package directions.
9. Serve the shrimp curry over the cauliflower rice.
10. Top with the fresh basil and serve with lime wedges.

Bunless Burgers with Ketchup

| Prep time: 10 minutes | Cook time: 10 minutes | Servings: 4 |

Ingredients for the ketchup

- o Unsulfured golden raisins – 1 tbsp.
- o Roasted red peppers – ½ (7 ounces) jar, drained
- o Extra-virgin olive oil – 3 tbsp.
- o Cider vinegar – 2 tbsp.
- o Tomato paste – 2 tbsp.
- o Salt – ¼ tsp.
- o Ground chipotle pepper – ¼ tsp.

For the burgers

- o Extra-virgin olive oil – 1 tbsp.
- o Ground beef – 1 pound
- o Salt – ½ tsp.

- Black pepper – ½ tsp.
- Dill pickles

Method

1. To make the ketchup: Add 2 tbsp. hot water and raisins in a blender. Let stand for 5 minutes.
2. Add the ground chipotle, salt, tomato paste, vinegar, oil, and roasted peppers. Cover and blend until smooth. Keep in the refrigerator.
3. Make the burgers: heat the olive oil in a skillet over medium heat.
4. Shape the meat into ¾-inch thick patties.
5. Season with salt and pepper.
6. Cook for 8 minutes, or until the internal temperature is 160F. Turning once.
7. Serve the patties with red-pepper ketchup.

Salmon Fillets with Pineapple

| Prep time: 5 minutes | Cook time: 15 minutes | Servings: 4 |

Ingredients

- Butter or ghee – 2 tbsp.
- Pineapple rings – 4, halved
- Minced fresh ginger – 1 tsp.
- Sesame seeds – ½ tsp.
- Skin on salmon fillets – 4 (5 to 6 ounces each)
- Salt – ½ tsp.
- Coconut oil – 1 tbsp.
- Black pepper – ¼ tsp.
- Chopped green onion

Method

1. Heat the butter over medium heat in a large skillet.

2. Add the ginger, sesame seeds, and pineapple. Cook for 6 to 8 minutes or until the pineapple is golden. Turning once. Transfer to a plate and keep warm. Wipe out the skillet.

3. Sprinkle the salmon with the salt and pepper.

4. Heat the same pan over medium heat.

5. Add the coconut oil and heat.

6. Place the salmon in the skillet, skin side down.

7. Cook, without touching for 4 to 5 minutes.

8. Then flip the salmon and cook for 2 to 3 minutes.

9. Serve the salmon with the caramelized pineapple.

Sweet and Spicy Chorizo with Spinach

| Prep time: 15 minutes | Cook time: 20 minutes | Servings: 2 |

Ingredients

- Coconut oil – 2 tbsp.
- Sweet potatoes - 3 medium, peeled and cut into ½ inch cubes
- Medium yellow onion – 1, diced
- Red bell pepper – 1 large, diced
- Garlic – 1 clove, minced
- Cooked chorizo links – ½ pound, halved lengthwise and diced
- Loosely packed baby spinach – 4 cups
- Fresh cilantro – ¼ cup

Method

1. Heat the coconut oil in a large skillet over medium heat.
2. Add the sweet potatoes and cook, covered for 5 minutes.
3. Uncover. Cook and stir for 5 to 8 minutes or until the potatoes are just tender.
4. Add the pepper and onion. Cook and stir for 5 minutes.
5. Add the spinach, chorizo, and garlic. Cook and stir occasionally for 4 minutes or until the spinach is wilted and chorizo is heated through.
6. Stir in the cilantro and serve.

Spicy Mussels with Squash

| Prep time: 20 minutes | Cook time: 10 minutes | Servings: 4 |

Ingredients

- Extra-virgin olive oil – 2 tbsp.
- Medium shallots – 4, finely chopped
- Garlic – 4 cloves, minced
- Diced tomatoes – 1 can (28 ounces)
- Red pepper flakes – ½ to 1 tsp.
- Salt – ½ tsp.
- Black pepper – ½ tsp.
- Mussels – 2 pounds, scrubbed and debearded
- Medium yellow summer squash – 2, trimmed and shaved into ribbons

- Fresh lemon juice – 2 tbsp.
- Chopped fresh basil – ½ cup

Method

1. Heat 1 tbsp. olive oil in a skillet over medium heat.
2. Add the garlic and shallot. Cook and stir for 2 minutes, or until softened.
3. Add the pepper flakes, tomatoes, salt, and pepper and bring to a boil.
4. Add the mussels. Cover and cook for 3 to 4 minutes, or until the mussels are just starting to open.
5. Stir in the squash ribbons.
6. Cook and stir occasionally for 1 to 2 minutes or until the squash is crisp-tender. Discard unopened mussels.
7. Drizzle the lemon juice and remaining 1 tbsp. olive oil over the mussels and squash.
8. Top with basil and serve.

Sweet Potato Noodles with Bacon and Eggs

| Prep time: 10 minutes | Cook time: 20 minutes | Servings: 2 |

Ingredients

- Whole30 compliant bacon – 4 slices
- Red onion – 1 small, chopped
- Butter or ghee – 2 tbsp.
- Sweet potatoes – 2 medium, peeled and spiralized
- Chopped fresh thyme – 2 tsp.
- Salt – ½ tsp.
- Black pepper – ½ tsp.
- Large eggs – 4

Method

1. Cook the bacon in a skillet over medium heat for 10 minutes or until crisp.
2. Transfer on paper towels to drain. Reserve 2 tbsp. of the dripping in the skillet.
3. Add the onion to the skillet and cook and stir for 3 minutes or until softened.
4. Add the butter and melt.
5. Add the sweet potato noodles and season with salt, pepper, and thyme.
6. Gently toss to combine.
7. Cook over medium heat for 5 minutes. Stirring occasionally.
8. Crumble the bacon and sprinkle over the noodles.

Skillet Butter Chicken

| Prep time: 15 minutes | Cook time: 20 minutes | Servings: 4 |

Ingredients

- Boneless, skillet chicken thighs – 1 ¼ pound, cut into 1-inch pieces
- Garam masala – 1 tbsp.
- Salt – ½ tsp.
- Cayenne pepper – 1/8 tsp.
- Butter or ghee – 2 tbsp.
- Medium onion – 1 chopped
- Garlic – 3 cloves, minced

- Minced fresh ginger – 1 tbsp.
- Coconut milk – 1 cup
- Diced tomatoes – 1 can (14.5 ounces), undrained
- Frozen riced cauliflower and sweet potato – 1 package (12 ounces)
- Chopped fresh cilantro – 2 tbsp.

Method

1. In a bowl, toss the chicken with garam masala, salt, and cayenne.
2. In a skillet, heat the butter over medium-high heat.
3. Add the chicken and cook for 4 to 6 minutes, or until browned. Stirring occasionally.
4. Stir in the onion. Cook and stir occasionally for 2 to 3 minutes.
5. Add the ginger and garlic. Cook and stir for 1 minute.
6. Stir in the diced tomatoes and juice and bring to a boil.
7. Lower the heat and simmer until the chicken is cooked through, about 10 to 12 minutes.
8. Stir in the coconut milk and cook for 1 minute.
9. Meanwhile, prepare the sweet potato and rice cauliflower according to package directions.
10. Spoon the butter chicken over the cooked cauliflower and sweet potato.
11. Top with cilantro and serve.

Turkey Meatballs with Tomatoes

| Prep time: 15 minutes | Roast time: 30 minutes | Servings: 3 |

Ingredients for the tomatoes

- Ground turkey – 1 ½ pound
- Large egg – 1
- Almond flour – ½ cup
- Garlic – 2 cloves, minced
- Italian seasoning – 2 tsp.
- Fennel seeds – 1 tsp. crushed
- Black pepper – 1 tsp.
- Salt – ½ tsp.

- Extra-virgin olive oil – 1 tbsp.

For the tomatoes

- Cherry tomatoes – 2 pint
- Extra-virgin olive oil – 1 tbsp.
- Garlic – 2 cloves, minced
- Italian seasoning – 1 tsp.
- Salt – ¼ tsp.
- Black pepper – ¼ tsp.
- Chopped fresh basil – 2 tbsp.

Method

1. Preheat the oven to 400F. Line a baking pan with parchment paper.
2. Make the meatballs: in a bowl, combine olive oil, salt, pepper, fennel seeds, Italian seasoning, garlic, almond flour, egg, and turkey. Make 9 meatballs.
3. Arrange the meatballs on the pan, spacing them evenly. Roast for 20 minutes.
4. Make the tomatoes: in a bowl, combine the garlic, Italian seasoning, olive oil, and cherry tomatoes. Season with the salt and black pepper.
5. Add the cherry tomatoes to the pan around the meatballs.
6. Turn the meatballs and roast until the internal temperature reaches 165F, about 10 minutes more.

7. Top the meatballs and roasted tomatoes with the fresh basil and serve.

Roasted Salmon with Tomatoes and Fennel

| Prep time: 20 minutes | Roast time: 15 minutes | Servings: 4 |

Ingredients

- Skin-on salmon fillet – 1 ½ pound
- Halved cherry tomatoes – 3 cups
- Medium fennel bulb – 1, thinly sliced
- Salt – ½ tsp.
- Black pepper – ½ tsp.
- Garlic – 2 cloves, minced
- Fresh lemon juice – 2 tbsp.
- Extra-virgin olive oil – 2 tbsp.
- Capers – 2 tbsp. drained
- Chopped fresh dill – 2 tsp.

- Dijon mustard – 2 tsp.

Method

1. Preheat the oven to 400F. Line a large baking pan with parchment paper.
2. Rinse the salmon and pat dry. Place the fennel, tomatoes, and salmon on the pan and sprinkle with salt and pepper.
3. In a bowl, stir together the mustard, dill, capers, olive oil, lemon juice, and garlic.
4. Drizzle the sauce over the fish and tomatoes. Stir to mix.
5. Roast the salmon for 15 to 18 minutes.
6. Serve.

Garlic Chicken with Bacon Cabbage

| Prep time: 20 minutes | Roast time: 35 minutes | Servings: 2 |

Ingredients

- o   Extra-virgin olive oil – 1 tbsp.
- o   Finely chopped fresh rosemary – 1 tbsp.
- o   Minced garlic – 2 tsp.
- o   Finely chopped fresh sage – 2 tsp.
- o   Grated zest of 1 lemon
- o   Coarse salt – 1 tsp.
- o   Black pepper – 1 tsp.
- o   Bone-in, skin-on chicken breasts – 2 (8 to 12 ounces each)
- o   Small green cabbage – ½, core intact, cut into 4 wedges
- o   Whole30 compliant bacon – 4 slices

- Fresh lemon juice

Method

1. Preheat the oven to 425F.
2. Combine the ½ tsp. black pepper, salt, lemon zest, sage, garlic, rosemary and olive oil in a bowl. Rub the chicken with the seasoning; over and underneath the skin.
3. Place the chicken, skin side up on a baking sheet and roast for 10 minutes.
4. Meanwhile, wrap each cabbage wedge with one slice of bacon.
5. Place the cabbage wedges on the other side of the baking pan.
6. Sprinkle with ½ tsp. black pepper.
7. Roast for 15 minutes or until the chicken reaches 170F and cabbage is tender.
8. Drizzle the chicken and cabbage with lemon juice and serve.

Kale, Potato Hash with Eggs

| Prep time: 20 minutes | Roast time: 30 minutes | Servings: 4 |

Ingredients

- Yukon Gold potatoes – 1 ½ pound, cut into ¾-inch pieces
- Large onion – 1, chopped
- Garlic – 3 cloves, chopped
- Extra-virgin olive oil – 3 tbsp.
- Dried oregano – 1 ½ tsp.
- Chili powder – 1 tsp.
- Coarse salt – 1 tsp.
- Black pepper – ½ tsp.

- Chopped kale – 4 cups
- Eggs – 8 large
- Green onions – 4, thinly sliced
- Chopped fresh parsley

Method

1. Place a rack in the center of the oven. Preheat the oven to 450F.
2. Line a large baking sheet with parchment paper.
3. In a bowl, combine the chili powder, salt, black pepper, oregano, olive oil, garlic, onion, and potatoes. Toss to coat.
4. Spread on the baking pan. Roast for 20 minutes or until the potatoes are just tender.
5. Lower the temperature to 400F.
6. Add the kale to the pan and stir until the kale wilts. If necessary, return the pan to the oven for a few minutes.
7. Make six indentations in the hash and break an egg into each indentation.
8. Roast for 8 to 10 minutes more or until the egg whites are set.
9. Top with the green onions, sprinkle with chopped parsley and serve.

Mushroom and Carrot Hash with Eggs

| Prep time: 15 minutes | Roast time: 30 minutes | Servings: 4 |

Ingredients

- Extra-virgin olive oil – 3 tbsp.
- Medium carrots – 3, peeled and chopped
- Medium parsnips – 3, peeled and chopped
- Medium red onion – 1, chopped
- Quartered button mushrooms – 2 cups
- Garlic – 2 cloves, minced
- Chili powder – 1 tsp.
- Ground cumin – ½ tsp.
- Smoked paprika – ½ tsp.
- Coarse salt – ½ tsp.
- Black pepper – ½ tsp.

- Large eggs – 8
- Torn fresh cilantro – 2 to 3 tbsp.

Method

1. Place a rack in the center of the oven.
2. Preheat the oven to 425F. Line a baking pan with parchment paper.
3. In a bowl, combine the cumin, smoked paprika, salt, black pepper, chili powder, garlic, mushrooms, onion, parsnips, carrots, and olive oil. Toss to coat.
4. Spread the mixture on the baking sheet and roast for 20 minutes.
5. Make four indentations in the hash and carefully break an egg into each indentation. Roast for 8 to 10 minutes more or until the egg whites are set.
6. Top with cilantro and serve.

Roasted Chicken Legs and Peppers

| Prep time: 10 minutes | Roast time: 35 minutes | Servings: 2 |

Ingredients

- Whole30 compliant, salt-free Cajun seasoning – 1 tbsp.
- Salt – ½ tsp.
- Chicken leg quarters – 2 (attached drumstick and thigh) 8 to 10 ounces each
- Extra-virgin olive oil – 2 tbsp.
- Fresh okra – 8 ounces
- Red bell pepper – 1 medium, coarsely chopped
- Medium onion – 1, chopped
- Celery – 1 stalk, diced
- Garlic – 4 cloves, minced
- Dried thyme – 1 tsp.
- Black pepper – ½ tsp.

- Chopped fresh parsley – ¼ cup

Method

1. Preheat the oven to 425F.
2. Combine the salt and seasoning in a bowl. Rub the chicken with the seasoning.
3. Place the chicken on one side of a large baking pan. Drizzle with 1 tbsp. olive oil.
4. Roast for 15 minutes.
5. Meanwhile, combine the black pepper, thyme, garlic, celery, onion, bell pepper, and okra in a large bowl. Drizzle with the remaining 1 tbsp. of the olive oil and toss to coat.
6. Place the vegetable on the other side of the baking pan.
7. Roast until the chicken reaches 175F and vegetables are tender about 20 minutes.
8. Sprinkle with the parsley and serve.

Orange Salmon with Herbed Sweet Potato Fries

| Prep time: 10 minutes | Bake time: 25 minutes | Servings: 4 |

Ingredients for the fries

- Sweet potatoes – 1 ½ pound, cut into ½ inch thick sticks
- Extra-virgin olive oil – 3 tbsp.
- Dried oregano – 1 tsp.
- Garlic powder – 1 tsp.
- Rosemary – 1 tsp. crushed
- Salt – 1 tsp.
- Black pepper – ½ tsp.
- Dried thyme – ½ tsp.

For the salmon

- Grated zest and juice of 2 mandarin oranges
- Ground ancho chili powder – 2 tsp.
- Dried oregano – 1 tsp.
- Garlic powder – ½ tsp.
- Salt – ½ tsp.
- Skin-on salmon fillet – 4 (4 to 6 ounces each)

Method

1. Preheat the oven to 425F. Line a large baking pan with parchment paper.
2. Make the fries: combine the thyme, pepper, salt, rosemary, garlic powder, oregano, olive oil, and sweet potatoes. Toss to coat.
3. Arrange the fries in a single layer on one side of the pan. Roast for 12 minutes.
4. For the salmon: Meanwhile, combine the salt, garlic powder, oregano, chili powder, and zest. Rub onto salmon fillets.
5. Place the fillets on the other side of the pan.
6. Bake for 12 to 15 minutes.
7. Drizzle the orange juice over the salmon and serve.

Salmon with Asparagus

| Prep time: 15 minutes | Roast time: 20 minutes | Servings: 4 |

Ingredients

- Extra-virgin olive oil – 2 tbsp.
- Fresh lemon juice – 1 tbsp.
- Coconut aminos – 1 tbsp.
- Rice vinegar – 2 tsp.
- Minced fresh ginger – 2 tsp.
- Garlic - 1 clove, minced
- Salt – ¼ tsp.
- Black pepper – ¼ tsp.
- Asparagus – 1 pound, trimmed

- Skin-on salmon fillets – 4 (6 ounces each)
- Lemon – 4 thin slices
- Sliced green onions
- Lemon wedges

Method

1. Preheat the oven to 425F. Line a large baking sheet with parchment paper.
2. In a bowl, stir together the ginger, garlic, salt, pepper, rice vinegar, coconut aminos, lemon juice, and olive oil.
3. In a large bowl, toss the asparagus with half of the dressing. Arrange the asparagus in a single layer on the pan and roast for 5 minutes.
4. Place the salmon fillets on top of the asparagus (skin side down). Top each fillet with a lemon slice.
5. Spoon the remaining dressing over the salmon and lemon.
6. Roast the salmon and asparagus for 15 minutes.
7. Serve with the green onions and lemon wedges.

Roasted Pork Chops with Green Onions

| Prep time: 15 minutes | Roast time: 25 minutes | Servings: 4 |

Ingredients

- Extra-virgin olive oil – 2 tbsp.
- Green onions – 2 bunches, trimmed and cut into 2-inch pieces
- Fresh sage leaves – 20, chopped
- Salt – 1 tsp.
- Ground black pepper – ¾ tsp.
- Minced fresh thyme – 2 tsp.
- Grated lemon zest – 1 tsp.
- Bone-in pork chops – 4 (3/4 to 1-inch thick) total 2 pounds

- Peeled and chopped butternut squash – 1 ½ pound

Method

1. Place the oven rack in the center of the oven and preheat the oven to 400F. Brush a large baking pan with 1 tbsp. olive oil.

2. Arrange the green onions on the pan to cover. Sprinkle the sage on top of the green onions.

3. In a bowl, combine the lemon zest, the thyme, ½ tsp. pepper, and ½ tsp. salt. Season the chops with the mixture. Place the chops on one side of the pan.

4. In a large bowl, combine the squash with the remaining ¼ tsp. pepper, ½ tsp. salt and 1 tbsp. olive oil. Toss to coat. Place the squash on the other half of the pan.

5. Roast the pork and squash for 20 minutes.

6. Then turn on the broiler and broil 4 inches from the heat source for 5 minutes or until the pork reaches 145F.

7. Rest the pork for 5 minutes and serve.

Shrimp with Broccoli

| Prep time: 10 minutes | Roast time: 35 minutes | Servings: 2 |

Ingredients

- Broccoli florets – 4 cups
- Toasted sesame oil – 2 tsp.
- Salt – 1/8 tsp.
- Red pepper flakes – 1/8 tsp.
- Lemon – 1, thinly sliced
- Extra-large shrimp – 12 ounces, peeled and deveined
- Garlic – 2 cloves, minced
- Butter or ghee – 2 tbsp. melted
- Coconut aminos – 1 tbsp.

Method

1. Preheat the oven to 400F. Line a baking pan with parchment paper.

2. In a bowl, toss together the broccoli, pepper flakes, salt, and sesame oil.

3. Spread the broccoli and lemon slices on one side of the pan.

4. Roast until the broccoli starts to brown, about 20 to 25 minutes.

5. Stir the broccoli and turn the lemon slices over.

6. Meanwhile, in the same bowl, toss together the coconut aminos, butter, garlic, and shrimp.

7. Add the shrimp in a single layer to the other half of the pan.

8. Roast the broccoli, shrimp and lemon slices until the shrimp are opaque, about 8 to 12 minutes.

9. Serve.

Cod with Zucchini and Brussels Sprouts

| Prep time: 20 minutes | Roast time: 20 minutes | Servings: 4 |

Ingredients

- Cod fillets – 4 (6 ounces each) rinse and pat dry
- Salt – ¾ tsp.
- Black pepper – ¾ tsp.
- Small zucchini – 2 to 3, ends trimmed,
- Avocado oil – 3 tbsp.
- Lemon – 8 slices
- Fresh thyme leaves – 1 tsp.
- Brussels sprouts – 4 cups, trimmed and halved

Method

1. Preheat the oven to 400F. Line a baking pan with parchment paper.
2. Sprinkle the cod with ½ tsp. salt and ½ tsp. black pepper.
3. Slice the zucchini into 1/16 inch thick ribbons. Wrap the ribbons around the fillets.
4. Place the cod on one side of the baking pan and drizzle with 1 tbsp. of the oil.
5. Place two lemon slices on top of each fillet and sprinkle with the thyme.
6. In a bowl, drizzle the Brussels sprouts with the remaining ¼ tsp. black pepper, ¼ tsp. salt and 2 tbsp. oil. Toss to coat.
7. Place the Brussels sprouts, cut side down on the other half of the pan.
8. Roast for 15 to 20 minutes and serve.

Shrimp and Chicken with Peppers

| Prep time: 15 minutes | Roast time: 15 minutes | Servings: 4 |

Ingredients

- Extra virgin olive oil – 2 tbsp.
- Chili powder – 2 tsp.
- Salt – 1 tsp.
- Ground cumin – ½ tsp.
- Ground cayenne – 1/8 tsp.
- Boneless, skinless chicken breasts – 1 pound, cut into ½ inch slices
- Red onion – 1, sliced
- Peeled and deveined medium shrimp – 1 ½ pound
- Lime wedges
- Chopped fresh cilantro

Method

1. Preheat the oven to 425F.
2. In a bowl, stir together the cayenne, cumin, salt chili powder, and olive oil.
3. Add the onion, bell peppers and chicken. Toss to coat.
4. Arrange the vegetables and chicken on a large baking pan. Bake for 10 minutes.
5. Stir the shrimp into the chicken and vegetables.
6. Roast for 5 to 6 minutes or until the shrimp is opaque.
7. Serve with lemon wedges and cilantro.

Sausage with Roasted Cabbage and Potatoes

| Prep time: 10 minutes | Roast time: 25 minutes | Servings: 4 |

Ingredients

- Butter or ghee – 2 tbsp.
- Dijon mustard – 2 tsp.
- Garlic – 2 cloves, minced
- Salt – ½ tsp.
- Black pepper – ¼ tsp.
- Green cabbage – 1 medium heat, core intact, cut into 8 wedges
- Red potatoes – 8, small, halved
- Whole30 compliant chicken and apple sausage – 2 packages (12 ounces each)

Method

1. Preheat the oven to 425F.
2. In a large bowl, stir together the salt, pepper, garlic, mustard, and butter.
3. Add the potatoes and cabbage and gently coat.
4. Arrange the vegetables and sausages on a baking pan.
5. Roast for 25 to 30 minutes, or until vegetables are tender and browned. Turning once.

Pork Tenderloin with Carrots

| Prep time: 10 minutes | Roast time: 40 minutes | Servings: 4 |

Ingredients

- Whole30 compliant coarse-grain mustard – ¼ cup
- Finely chopped fresh parsley – 1 tbsp.
- Black pepper – 1 tsp.
- Salt – 1 tsp.
- Grated lemon zest – ½ tsp.
- Pork tenderloin - 1 (1 ¼ pound)
- Baby carrots – 1 bag (16 ounces)
- Sweet onion – 1 medium, cut into thin wedges
- Avocado or olive oil – 2 tbsp.
- Finely chopped fresh rosemary – 1 tbsp.
- Garlic – 2 cloves, minced

Method

1. Preheat the oven to 425F. Line a baking pan with parchment paper.

2. In a bowl, stir together the lemon zest, ½ tsp. salt, parsley, pepper, and mustard.

3. Spread the mixture all over the tenderloin. Place the tenderloin on the pan.

4. In a bowl, toss the onion and carrots, with the rosemary, oil, garlic, and ½ tsp. salt. Place the vegetables around the tenderloin.

5. Roast the tenderloin at 145F for 25 to 30 minutes or until it reaches 145F.

6. Transfer the pork to a cutting board and cover with foil.

7. Continue to roast the vegetables for 10 more minutes or until tender.

8. Slice the pork and serve with vegetables.

Buffalo Chicken with Cauliflower

| Prep time: 10 minutes | Roast/Cook time: 35 minutes | Servings: 2 |

Ingredients

- Cauliflower florets – 4 cups
- Extra-virgin olive oil – 1 tbsp.
- Salt – ¼ tsp.
- Black pepper – 1/8 tsp.
- Butter or ghee – 2 tbsp. melted
- Boneless, skinless, chicken breasts - 2
- Whole30 compliant buffalo sauce – 2 tbsp. plus more for serving
- Whole30 ranch dressing – ¼ cup

Method

1. Preheat the oven to 425F. Line a large baking pan with parchment paper.

2. In a large bowl, combine olive oil, cauliflower, salt, and pepper. Mix well.

3. Spread the cauliflower on one part of the pan and roast for 15 minutes.

4. Meanwhile, heat 1 tbsp. butter in a skillet over medium heat. Add the chicken and cook for 5 to 6 minutes, or until golden brown. Turning once.

5. In the same bowl, stir together the remaining 1 tbsp. butter and the buffalo sauce. Add the browned chicken and coat with sauce.

6. Add the chicken to the pan. Roast for 20 to 25 minutes longer or until the chicken reaches 170F.

7. Serve the cauliflower and the chicken with the ranch dressing for dipping.

8. Drizzle the chicken with additional buffalo sauce and serve.

Chapter 7 Side Dishes

Roasted Brussels Sprouts

| Prep time: 10 minutes | Roast time: 10 minutes | Servings: 2 |

Ingredients

- Brussels sprouts – 2 cups, trimmed and halved
- Butter or ghee – 2 tbsp. melted
- Paprika – 1 tsp.
- Red pepper flakes – ½ to 1 tsp.
- Salt – ¼ tsp.
- Black pepper – ¼ tsp.
- Fresh lemon juice – 2 tsp.
- Whole30 compliant tahini – 2 tbsp.

Method

1. Preheat the oven to 400F. Line a baking sheet with parchment paper.

2. In a bowl, combine the butter, Brussels sprouts, paprika, pepper flakes, salt, and black pepper. Place the Brussels sprouts in a single layer on the pan.

3. Roast the Brussels sprouts for 8 to 10 minutes. Stirring once halfway through cooking.

4. Drizzle the lemon juice over the Brussels sprouts and serve with the tahini for dipping.

Chili-Lime Roasted Sweet Potatoes

Prep time: 5 minutes	Roast time: 20 minutes	Servings: 4

Ingredients

- Frozen cubed sweet potatoes – 1 bag (16 ounces)
- Coconut oil – 2 tbsp. melted
- Jalapeno – ½, finely chopped
- Ground cumin – 1 tsp.
- Salt – ½ tsp.
- Lime wedges

Method

1. Preheat the oven to 450F. Line a large baking sheet with parchment paper.

2. Place the sweet potatoes in a medium bowl. Cover with microwave-safe plastic wrap; pull back a small section of the plastic wrap so the steam can escape. Microwave on high temperature for 2 minutes.

3. Add the salt, cumin, jalapeno and coconut oil and toss to coat.

4. Place the sweet potatoes on the pan and roast for 20 minutes, or until golden. Stirring once halfway through.

5. Serve with the lime wedges.

Veggie confetti Cauliflower-Rice

| Prep time: 10 minutes | Cook time: 10 minutes | Servings: 5 |

Ingredients

- Butter or ghee – 3 tbsp.
- Finely diced yellow onion – ½ cup
- Finely diced cremini mushrooms – ½ cup
- Finely diced carrot – ¼ cup
- Finely diced red bell pepper – ¼ cup
- Finely diced zucchini – ¼ cup
- Salt – ¾ tsp.
- Dried parsley – ½ tsp.
- Garlic powder – ½ tsp.
- Black pepper – ¼ tsp.
- Cauliflower crumbles – 1 package (16 ounces)

- Chicken broth – 1/3 cup

Method

1. Heat the butter in a skillet over medium heat.
2. Add the zucchini, bell pepper, carrot, mushrooms, and onion.
3. Cook for 5 minutes or until vegetables are softened. Stirring occasionally.
4. Add the black pepper, garlic powder, parsley, and salt. Cook and stir until combined.
5. Stir in the cauliflower.
6. Cook for 2 to 3 minutes. Stirring occasionally.
7. Add the broth and cook for 2 minutes or until the cauliflower is just tender.
8. Fluff with a fork and serve.

Quick Beet and Cabbage Salad

| Prep time: 10 minutes | Total time: 10 minutes | Servings: 4 |

Ingredients

- Whole beets – 1 can (15 ounces), drained
- Shredded red cabbage – 1 bag (10 ounces)
- Finely chopped shallot – 1/3 cup
- Dried dark sweet cherries – ½ cup, chopped
- Roasted salted sunflower seeds – ¼ cup
- Chopped fresh parsley – ¼ cup
- Red wine vinegar – 3 tbsp.
- Balsamic vinegar – 1 tbsp.
- Extra-virgin olive oil – ¼ cup
- Salt – ¼ tsp.
- Black pepper – ¼ tsp.

Method

1. Slice the beets and cut into thin strips.
2. Combine the parsley, sunflower seeds, cherries, shallot, cabbage, and beets in a bowl.
3. Drizzle with both of the vinegars and toss to coat.
4. Drizzle with the olive oil, sprinkle with the salt and black pepper. Toss to coat.
5. Serve.

Lemon – Dill Parsnips

| Prep time: 20 minutes | Roast time: 20 minutes | Servings: 4 |

Ingredients

- Parsnips – 2 pounds, peeled and cut into matchsticks
- Extra-virgin olive oil – 3 tbsp.
- Garlic – 3 cloves, thinly sliced
- Salt – ½ tsp.
- Black pepper – 1/8 tsp.
- Fresh lemon juice – 2 tbsp.
- Snipped fresh dill – 2 tsp.

Method

1. Preheat the oven to 425F.
2. Combine the olive oil, parsnips, garlic, salt and pepper in a bowl. Toss to coat.

3. Place the parsnips in an even layer on two baking sheets.

4. Roast, uncovered, for 20 to 30 minutes or until starting to brown. Stirring twice.

5. Drizzle with the lemon juice and sprinkle with dill.

6. Toss and serve.

Herbed Celery Root Fries with Lemon Aioli

| Prep time: 20 minutes | Roast time: 25 minutes | Servings: 2 |

Ingredients

- Celery root without tops – 1 pound, cut into ½ inch thick fries
- Extra-virgin olive oil – 3 tbsp.
- Herbs de Provence – 2 tsp.
- Salt – ½ tsp.
- Black pepper – ½ tsp.
- Mayonnaise – ½ cup
- Grated lemon zest – ½ tsp.
- Fresh lemon juice – 1 tbsp.
- Garlic – 1 clove, minced

Method

1. Preheat the oven to 450F.
2. Place the celery root fries in a bowl. Drizzle with olive oil and sprinkle with black pepper, salt, and herbs. Toss to coat.
3. Place the fries in an even layer on a large baking sheet. Roast, for 25 minutes, or until tender and golden. Stirring once.
4. Meanwhile, for the aioli, combine the garlic, lemon zest and juice, and mayonnaise.
5. Serve fries with aioli.

Green Beans with Toasted Almonds

| Prep time: 5 minutes | Cook time: 8 minutes | Servings: 4 |

Ingredients

- Coconut oil – 1 tbsp.
- Fresh green beans – 1 pound, trimmed
- Grated lemon zest – 1 tsp.
- Fresh lemon juice – 1 to 2 tsp.
- Salt – ¼ tsp.
- Black pepper – ¼ tsp.
- Sliced almonds – ¼ cup, toasted

Method

1. Heat the coconut oil in a skillet over medium heat.

2. Add the green beans and cook without stirring for 2 minutes.

3. Stir and continue to cook for 5 to 6 minutes. Stirring occasionally.

4. Remove the skillet from the heat and stir in the lemon zest, juice, salt, and black pepper.

5. Sprinkle with almonds and serve.

Sautéed Sugar Snap Peas

| Prep time: 5 minutes | Cook time: 5 minutes | Servings: 2 |

Ingredients

- Butter or ghee – 1 tbsp.
- Finely chopped shallot – 2 tbsp.
- Minced fresh ginger – 1 tsp.
- Red pepper flakes – 1/8 tsp.
- Fresh stringless sugar snap peas – 1 bag (8 ounces)
- Coconut amions – 2 tsp.

Method

1. Heat the butter in a medium skillet over medium heat.

2. Add the pepper flakes, ginger, and shallot. Cook and stir for 1 minute.

3. Add the sugar snap peas and cook until crisp-tender, 3 to 5 minutes longer.

4. Stir in coconut aminos and serve.

Roasted Whole Cauliflower

| Prep time: 10 minutes | Roast time: 1 hour | Servings: 4 |

Ingredients

- Medium heat cauliflower – 1
- Water – ½ cup
- Extra-virgin olive oil – 2 tbsp.
- Salt – ½ tsp.
- Black pepper – ¼ tsp.
- Garlic – 3 cloves, thinly sliced
- Chopped fresh basil or parsley – 2 tbsp.
- Chopped fresh oregano – 2 tsp.

Method

1. Preheat the oven to 400F.

2. Trim the leaves and leave the head intact. Place the cauliflower, stem side down in an 8 x 8-inch square baking dish. Add the water to the dish and cover tightly with foil. Roast for 30 minutes.

3. Remove the foil. Brush the cauliflower with olive oil and sprinkle with salt and black pepper.

4. Insert the garlic slices between the grooves on the cauliflower.

5. Roast the cauliflower, uncovered for 30 minutes.

6. In a small bowl, combine the basil and oregano.

7. Cut the cauliflower into wedges. Sprinkle with the fresh herbs and serve.

Cauliflower Sweet Potato Mash

| Prep time: 5 minutes | Cook time: 15 minutes | Servings: 4 |

Ingredients

- Sweet potatoes – 1 pound, peeled and chopped
- Cauliflower florets – 3 cups
- Garlic – 2 cloves, peeled
- Butter or ghee – 3 tbsp.
- Salt -1/2 tsp.
- Black pepper – ¼ tsp.

Method

1. In a large saucepan, place the garlic, cauliflower, and sweet potatoes. Add enough water to cover and bring to boil.

2. Lower the heat, cover and simmer for 12 to 15 minutes. Drain.

3. Mash the vegetables with a potato masher.

4. Stir in the butter, salt, and pepper.

5. Serve.

Scramble Eggs

| Prep time: 15 minutes | Cook time: 5 to 7 minutes | Servings: 2 |

Ingredients

- Avocado – 1, split lengthwise, pitted and peeled, cut into thin slices
- Cooking fat – 2 tbsp.
- Eggs – 6 large, beaten
- Salt – 1 tsp.
- Black pepper – ½ tsp.

- Salsa – 1 cup

Method

1. Heat the cooking fat in a skillet over medium heat.
2. In a bowl, whisk the eggs with salt and pepper.
3. Add the eggs in the hot oil and cook for 5 to 7 minutes or until eggs are scrambled and fluffy. Stirring occasionally.
4. Divide the eggs between 2 plates. Top with avocado and salsa.

Greek Salad

| Prep time: 15 minutes | Cook time: 0 minutes | Servings: 2 |

Ingredients

- Romaine lettuce – 1 head, chopped
- Tomatoes – 4, seeded and cut into large dice
- Cucumber – 1, peeled and cut into large dice
- Red onion – ½, thinly sliced
- Pitted Kalamata olives – 30, halved
- Extra-virgin olive oil – ¼ cup
- Red wine vinegar – 2 tbsp.
- Garlic – 1 clove, minced

- Salt – ¼ tsp.
- Black pepper – ¼ tsp.
- Juice of ½ lemon

Method

1. In a bowl, combine the olives, onion, cucumber, tomatoes, and lettuce.
2. Combine the salt, pepper, garlic, vinegar and olive oil in another bowl and whisk.
3. Pour the dressing over the salad ingredients and top with the lemon juice.

Green Cabbage Slaw

| Prep time: 20 minutes | Cook time: 0 minutes | Servings: 2 |

Ingredients

- Garlic – 1 clove, minced
- Juice of 1 lemon
- Extra-virgin olive oil – ¼ cup
- Green cabbage – 1 medium head, finely shredded
- Shredded carrots – 1 cup
- Chopped cashews – 2 tbsp.
- Sesame seeds – 1 tsp.
- Salt – ½ tsp.
- Black pepper – ½ tsp.
- Chopped fresh basil – 1 tbsp.

Method

1. In a bowl, whisk the garlic and lemon juice. Whisk and slowly add the oil until mixed.

2. In a large bowl, combine the sesame seeds, cashews, carrots, and cabbage. Mix and then toss with the lemon oil. Adjust the seasoning with the salt and pepper and top with basil.

3. Serve.

Roasted Root Vegetables in Curry Sauce

| Prep time: 15 minutes | Cook time: 35 minutes | Servings: 2 |

Ingredients

- Peeled, diced potato – 1 cup
- Peeled, diced rutabaga – 1 cup
- Peeled, diced turnips – 1 cup
- Peeled, diced parsnips – 1 cup
- Peeled diced carrots – 1 cup
- Cooking fat – ¼ cup
- Curry sauce – ½ cup

Method

1. Preheat the oven to 400F. Line 2 baking sheets with parchment paper.

2. Melt the cooking fat and combine with all the vegetables in a bowl. Mix well.

3. Spread the vegetables in one layer on the 2 baking sheets.

4. Roast for 30 to 40 minutes or until they are fork-tender.

5. Serve topped with curry sauce.

Roasted Spaghetti Squash

Prep time: 10 minutes	Cook time: 1 hour	Servings: 2

Ingredients

- Spaghetti squash – 1 whole
- Extra-virgin olive oil – 2 tbsp.
- Fresh thyme leaves – 2 tsp.
- Salt – ½ tsp.
- Black pepper – ¼ tsp.

Method

1. Preheat the oven to 425F. Line a baking sheet with foil or parchment paper.
2. Cut the squash in half lengthwise and remove the seeds. Drizzle the insides with olive oil. Place the squash flesh-side on the baking side.
3. Roast the squash for 1 hour or until fork-tender.
4. Flip and cool.
5. Then gently scrape out the flesh with a fork. Make it a noodle like strands.
6. Season with salt, pepper, and thyme.
7. Serve.

Chapter 8 Dessert Recipes

Strawberries in Coconut Cream

| Prep time: 10 minutes | Cook time: 20 minutes | Servings: 4 |

Ingredients

- o Full fat coconut milk – 1 can, cooled
- o Strawberries – 2 pints, quartered, and divided
- o Coconut oil – 1 tbsp.
- o Balsamic vinegar – 1 tbsp.

- Honey – 1 tbsp.

Method

1. Preheat the oven to 400F.
2. Line a baking sheet with parchment paper and set aside.
3. In a bowl, add 1-cup berries with vinegar and coconut oil. Mix.
4. Spread on the baking sheet and roast for 15 to 20 minutes. Cool.
5. Mix roasted berries with fresh berry juice. Add honey and mix.
6. Add cooled, thick coconut cream (from the can) into a chilled bowl.
7. Mix with a hand blender until creamy.
8. Coconut cream and berries in a small bowl.
9. Serve.

Dessert Bites

| Prep time: 20 minutes | Cook time: 0 minute | Servings: 5 |

Ingredients

- Coconut butter – ¼ cup
- Almond butter – 2 tbsp.
- Almond extract – ¼ tsp.
- Pinch of salt

Optional

- Cocoa powder – 1 tsp. unsweetened
- Coconut oil – ½ tbsp.

Method

1. In a bowl, combine the almond and coconut butter and melt in a microwave.
2. Mix to make it smooth.
3. Add salt and almond extract and mix again.
4. Freeze for 10 minutes.
5. Then roll into balls and freeze again for 5 minutes.
6. Melt the optional coconut oil and then mix with cocoa powder.
7. Dip the balls in the mixture and set aside to set.
8. Serve.

Ice Cream

| Prep time: 480 minutes | Cook time: 15 minutes | Servings: 4 |

Ingredients

- Bananas – 4, (2 sliced and frozen overnight, the other 2 are sliced)
- Butter – 3 tbsp. salted

- Coconut milk – ½ cup, chilled
- Pecans – ½ cup, chopped and toasted

Method

1. Melt the butter in a pan.
2. Place the unfrozen banana slices in the pan with the butter and cook until golden brown on both sides.
3. Remove all the butter and bananas from the pan and place in a container.
4. Freeze overnight.
5. Place both cooked and uncooked bananas in a blender and blend.
6. Then add the coconut milk and blend until very smooth.
7. Add the pecans and mix with a spoon.
8. Serve.

Caramelized Pears and Apples with Coconut Butter

Prep time: 2 minutes	Cook time: 7 minutes	Servings: 3

Ingredients

- Large apple – 1, peeled and sliced
- Large pear – 1, peeled and sliced (not too ripe)
- Coconut oil – 2 tbsp. more if needed
- Ground cinnamon – 2 tsp.
- Sea salt – ¼ tsp.
- Coconut butter – 3 tbsp. melted

Method

1. Heat 1 tbsp. coconut oil in a nonstick skillet.
2. Add the sliced apples. Cook and stir for 1 minute, then add the pears and combine.
3. Season with salt. Cook and stir for 3 minutes, or until softened. Add more oil and adjust heat if needed.
4. Lower the heat to low and season with cinnamon. Mix.
5. Once cooked, remove from the heat.
6. Melt the coconut butter in the microwave.
7. Drizzle over apples and pears.
8. Serve.

Chocolate Cupcakes

Prep time: 5 minutes	Cook time: 15 to 18 minutes	Servings: 12 mini muffins

Ingredients

- Ripe bananas – 2, peeled
- Apple – 1, peeled and chopped
- Dates – 5 to 6
- Eggs – 2 large
- Almond butter – 1 cup
- Cocoa powder – ¼ cup
- Baking soda – 1 ¼ tsp.
- Cinnamon – 1 tsp.
- Pinch of sea salt

Method

1. Preheat the oven to 375F.
2. Place all the ingredients in the blender and blend for 2 minutes.
3. Fill cupcake liners ¾ full.
4. Bake in the oven for 15 to 18 minutes.
5. Check after 15 minutes.
6. Cool and serve.

Chia Pudding

| Prep time: 5 minutes | Cook time: 8 hours | Servings: 4 |

Ingredients

- Coconut milk – 2 (14-ounce) cans
- Chia seeds – ¼ cup
- More coconut milk for thinning
- Ripe bananas – 2, sliced
- Roasted sliced almonds – ½ cup

Method

1. Open the cans and pour the milk into a bowl. Mix the cream and liquid.

2. Now add chia seeds and mix well. Cover and refrigerate for 8 to 12 hours.

3. Before dessert time, add chia pudding in serving bowls.

4. Add more coconut milk if necessary.

5. Top with toasted almonds and sliced bananas and serve.

Creamy Bowls

| Prep time: 15 minutes | Cook time: 0 minute | Servings: 2 to 4 |

Ingredients

- Cantaloupe – 1 (3 to 4 pounds) seeds removed and sliced into quarters
- Ripe bananas – 2, sliced and frozen
- Strawberries – 1 cup, quartered
- Vanilla extract – 1 tsp.
- Almond extract – ¼ tsp.

Toppings

- Sliced strawberries – 2 cups
- Fresh raspberries – 1 cup

- Shredded coconut – 2 tbsp. unsweetened

Method

1. Place each melon piece in a bowl and set aside.
2. Add frozen banana slices, almond extract, strawberries, and vanilla extract in a food processor and process until smooth.
3. Spoon the mixture into the cantaloupe pieces.
4. Top with toppings and serve.

Brownies

| Prep time: 10 minutes | Cook time: 20 minutes | Servings: 4 |

Ingredients

- Ripe bananas – 3
- Creamy almond butter – ½ cup, salted
- 100% cocoa powder – 2 tbsp.

Method

1. Preheat the oven to 350F.
2. Lightly on a baking pan (7 x 11).
3. Mix almond butter and banana until smooth.
4. Add the cocoa powder and mix well.

5. Pour batter into the pan.
6. Bake for 20 minutes.
7. Cool and serve.

Apple Parfait

| Prep time: 5 minutes | Cook time: 8 minutes | Servings: 4 |

Ingredients

- Coconut oil – 2 tbsp.
- Apples – 4 to 5, chopped
- Cinnamon – 1 tsp.
- Nutmeg – ¼ tsp.
- Walnuts – ¼ cup
- Pecans – ¼ cup
- Almonds – ¼ cup
- Dates – 4, chopped
- Nut butter – 1 to 2 tbsp.

Method

1. In a skillet, heat the oil over medium heat.
2. Add the chopped apples. Cook and stir for 2 minutes.
3. Then add the nutmeg and cinnamon.
4. Cook until apples are soft.
5. Remove the apples from heat and place in a bowl.
6. Add dates and nuts and mix.
7. Drizzle with nut butter and serve.

Cookies

Prep time: 10 minutes	Cook time: 15 minutes	Servings: 24 cookies

Ingredients

- Ripe banana pure – 1 ½ cups
- Peanut butter – ½ cup, unsweetened
- Cocoa powder – ½ cup
- Salt for garnish

Method

1. Preheat the oven to 350F.
2. Combine the first 3 ingredients in a bowl and mix with a fork until smooth.

3. Drop 1 tbsp. of the mixture on to a prepared cookie sheet (1 inch apart).

4. Sprinkle with salt.

5. Bake until cookies lose their sheen, about 8 to 15 minutes.

6. Cool and serve.

Cherry Chocolate Ice Cream

Prep time: 10 minutes	Cook time: 3 hours 15 minutes	Servings: 3

Ingredients

- Frozen cherries – 2 cups
- Banana – ½, frozen
- Almond milk – ½ cup, unsweetened, and divided
- Dairy-free chocolate chips – 3 tbsp.

Method

1. Froze ¼-cup almond milk in ice cube trays.

2. In a food processor, place the almond milk cubes, ¼ cup almond milk, frozen banana, and frozen cherries. Process until smooth.

3. Stir in the chocolate chips and serve.

Spinach Ice Cream

Prep time: 10 minutes	Cook time: 2 hours 15 minutes	Servings: 2

Ingredients

- Bananas – 2, sliced and frozen
- Mango chunks – ¾ cup, frozen
- Pineapple chunks – ¼ cup, frozen
- Spinach – 1 packed cup

- Vanilla soymilk – 1 tbsp.

Method

1. In a blender, place soymilk, spinach, pineapple, frozen mango, and frozen banana.
2. Blend until smooth.
3. Top with dark chocolate and serve.

Eggnog Smoothie

| Prep time: 10 minutes | Cook time: 0 minute | Servings: 2 |

Ingredients

- Almond milk – 3 cups
- Banana – 1
- Nutmeg – ½ tsp. freshly ground
- Almond extract – 1 tsp.
- Dates – 2, pitted

Method

1. Blend everything in a blender and serve.

Peanut Butter Ice Cream

| Prep time: 10 minutes | Cook time: 1 hour | Servings: 2 |

Ingredients

- Bananas – 2, peeled and frozen
- Peanut butter – 1 tbsp.

Method

1. Place the peanut butter and bananas in a food processor.
2. Blend well and serve.

Almond Butter Cookies

| Total time: 30 minutes | Servings: 24 |

Ingredients

- o   Ripe bananas – 2, mashed
- o   Almond flour – ½ cup
- o   Almond butter – ½ cup
- o   Cocoa powder – ¼ cup
- o   Raisins – ½ cup

Method

1. Preheat the oven to 350F.
2. Line two baking sheets with parchment paper and set aside.
3. Combine the cocoa, almond butter, almond flour, and bananas.
4. Mix until combined and stir in the raisins.
5. On the prepared baking sheets, drop chunks of batter (1-tbsp.).
6. Bake for 10 to 12 minutes.
7. Cool and serve.

Carrot Cake Cookies

| Prep time: 10 minutes | Cook time: 35 minutes | Servings: 5 |

Ingredients

- Mini carrots – 2 cups
- Almonds – 2 cups
- Shredded coconut – 1 cup
- Nutmeg – 1 tsp.
- Vanilla – 2 tsp.
- Coconut oil – 2 tsp.
- Eggs – 3

Method

1. Preheat the oven to 350F.

2. Except for the eggs, combine everything in a food processor. Process until mixed.

3. In a bowl, combine the mixture with the eggs.

4. Make 10 patties.

5. Bake for 35 to 40 minutes.

6. Serve.

Conclusion

The Whole30 is not another ordinary diet plan. With this eating plan, you won't be eating based on a points system or tracking calories. The diet will make you feel good and help you lose weight at the same time. Ideally, you should start this eating program with a friend to make it a success.

Made in the USA
Middletown, DE
10 February 2019